Royal Palaces

OF BRITAIN

Royal Palaces

OF BRITAIN

JANE STRUTHERS

Photography by CHRIS COE

& PAUL RIDDLE

NEW HOLLAND

First published in 2004 by New Holland Publishers (UK) Ltd
London • Cape Town • Sydney • Auckland

www.newhollandpublishers.com

Garfield House, 86–88 Edgware Road, London, W2 2EA, UK

80 McKenzie Street, Cape Town 8001, South Africa

Level 1/Unit 4, 14 Aquatic Drive, Frenchs Forest, NSW 2086, Australia

218 Lake Road, Northcote, Auckland, New Zealand

ISBN 1 84330 733 2

Publishing Manager: Jo Hemmings
Senior Editors: Jane Morrow, Charlotte Judet
Editor: Deborah Taylor
Designer: Gülen Shevki-Taylor
Production: Joan Woodroffe
Cartographer: William Smuts

Reproduction by Pica Digital Pte Ltd, Singapore
Printed and bound by Kyodo Printing Co Pte Ltd, Singapore

COVER AND PRELIM PAGES

FRONT COVER: Buckingham Palace has been a royal residence since George III bought it in 1761 as his family home.

BACK COVER, LEFT: The Drawing Room at Scone Palace is one of the many stunning interiors at this ancient Scottish seat.

BACK COVER, MIDDLE: Harlech Castle continues to dominate the town, over 700 years after it was built to subdue the Welsh.

BACK COVER, RIGHT: The Cupola Room in Kensington Palace is one of the many fascinating rooms in this London palace.

SPINE: The Tower of London has contained a fortress, prison, mint, menagerie, execution ground and palace in its time.

Page 2: The Ceremony of the Order of the Garter takes place each June at Windsor Castle, and dates from 1348.

OPPOSITE: Glamis Castle in Scotland has always been a family home, and the Drawing Room conveys this atmosphere.

Contents

INTRODUCTION

Britain is rich in historic buildings and some of the grandest and most fascinating of them all are the royal palaces and castles. All the properties that appear in this book are, at some point each year, open to the public. There is restricted entry to some of the working palaces, such as St James's Palace, but the public can still visit some areas at certain times of the year. Some of the properties are world-famous; others offer the visitor a chance to discover somewhere completely new. Most of the buildings can be easily categorized as either a castle or a palace; others, such as Windsor Castle, combine the two, with royal palaces contained within a fortified structure. A few, such as Althorp, are not strictly royal palaces or castles at all but have been included because of their strong connections with royalty.

Each one of the buildings featured has its own distinct history. Some of these histories are very private and only known to the people who live there; others are so important that they have found their way into the history books. In some cases we remember the story but not the building. In London, for example, thousands of commuters and tourists stream past the Banqueting House in Whitehall each day, most of them unaware that here, in the winter of 1649, Charles I was executed.

This book not only describes how and when the palaces were built, but it also tells the stories of those who lived in them. Some of Britain's monarchs have become so well known for a particular trait, quest or tragedy that it is difficult to look beyond it and to gain a more rounded understanding of them as human beings. Henry VIII is often regarded as a pantomime villain because of his treatment of his six wives and Queen Victoria is thought of as the classic Victorian widow, wallowing in grief after the death of her adored husband. Through the places in which they actually lived, however, this book shows that these people were as human as anyone else.

Many of the palaces and castles featured were heavily influenced by events that were taking place at the time that they were built. William the Conqueror's invasion of England in 1066, for example, sparked off an ambitious building programme of fortifications that were intended to secure his position as king – the Tower of London and Windsor Castle both date from this time. Edward I, in the late thirteenth century, had to quell uprisings in Wales so he built a ring of castles, including those at Caernarfon and Harlech. His similar problems in Scotland led to his involvement in the history of Edinburgh and Stirling Castles. In the 1520s, Henry VIII punished Cardinal Wolsey for failing to secure his first divorce by making him forfeit such buildings as Hampton Court and Whitehall Palace. The English Civil War in the 1640s led to many royal palaces and castles, including Chirk Castle and Linlithgow Palace, being confiscated by the Parliamentarians, who then either kept or sold off the contents before damaging the buildings themselves. Later still, when the Prince Regent was preparing for his reign as George IV in the early 1800s, royal properties were converted into suitably lavish palaces; among these were Windsor Castle and Buckingham Palace.

As a direct result of historical events, each building has acquired its own particular charm and character. Some of them are now cosy and welcoming homes, while others have retained the sense of awe and dignity that has always surrounded royalty.

Jane Struthers

Royal Palaces of Britain

1. Windsor Castle
2. Hampton Court Palace
3. Sandringham House
4. The Royal Pavilion
5. Osborne House
6. Hever Castle
7. Carisbrooke Castle
8. Hatfield Palace
9. Buckingham Palace
10. The Tower of London
11. Kensington Palace
12. St James's Palace
13. The Palace of Westminster
14. Eltham Palace
15. The Banqueting House
16. The Queen's House
17. Caernarfon Castle
18. Harlech Castle
19. Blenheim Palace
20. Chirk Castle
21. Berkeley Castle
22. Linlithgow Palace
23. Balmoral Castle
24. Falkland Palace
25. The Palace of Holyroodhouse
26. Glamis Castle
27. Edinburgh Castle
28. Stirling Castle
29. Traquair House
30. Scone Palace
31. Althorp

South East England and East Anglia

After the Normans invaded England in 1066, the architectural landscape of the country was changed forever. Castles sprang up like mushrooms, with the purpose of subduing the newly conquered English and also repelling hopeful foreign invaders. Windsor Castle, which is now one of the best known royal residences in the world, began life as a simple motte and bailey fort. Some of the buildings in this part of Britain were intended to be private homes to which members of royalty could retreat when necessary, and Sandringham House in Norfolk continues to fulfil this essential function.

RIGHT: *The Queen's Dining Room, at Osborne House on the Isle of Wight, has been restored to the full grandeur that it enjoyed when Queen Victoria lived here. Osborne was a treasured retreat from the pressures of state for Victoria and her consort, Prince Albert, and it became even more important for her after Albert died in 1861. It still retains the atmosphere of a much-loved family house.*

WINDSOR CASTLE

Windsor Castle enjoys several distinctions: it is the oldest occupied palace in Europe; the largest occupied castle in the world; and the Round Tower makes it one of the most easily recognized buildings in the world. The castle can be seen for miles around, thanks to its magnificent, strategic position atop a chalk ridge high above the Thames west of London. Today, Windsor Castle looks rather like a child's toy fort, albeit on a massive scale as the castle and its attendant buildings sprawl across 5 hectares (13 acres) of land.

Establishing a Motte and Bailey Castle

After William the Conqueror successfully invaded England in 1066, it was essential that he kept an iron grip on his new subjects and also repelled any other would-be invaders – to ensure this he built a series of castles that encircled London, including one at Windsor. The area around Windsor was already familiar to English kings because they hunted deer here, so by the time Henry II was on the throne in the twelfth century it made sense to build a royal palace at Windsor. Henry built rooms for the official side of palace life in the Lower Ward, and a set of private apartments in the Upper Ward. He was also responsible for replacing the original timber keep on top of the motte with one made of stone. This was the beginning of what is now the Round Tower.

The Order of the Garter

Although succeeding kings all made their mark on Windsor Castle, none had such an impact as Edward III, who was born here in 1312. Edward III financed the work on Windsor from his successful wars in France, turning it into a fortified palace in which he spent as much time as possible. Edward was also responsible for founding the Order of the Garter, which was based on the medieval ideals of chivalry. This is the oldest chivalric order in Britain, and it is still bestowed as a mark of royal favour. The first ceremony of the Garter was held on 23 April 1348, as it is the day of the festival of St George, the patron saint of England and also of soldiers. The existing King's Chapel was renamed St George's Chapel, and the Order's original insignia were a garter and badge showing St George and the dragon that he slew. The origins of the garter are uncertain, but a romantic legend has it that Edward was dancing with Joan, Countess of Salisbury, when her garter fell off. Edward picked it up and tied it to his own leg, much to the amusement of the onlookers. He is reputed to have said 'Honi soit qui mal y pense' ('Shame on him who thinks ill of this'), which became the motto of the Order.

St George's Chapel

In 1475, Edward IV commissioned Henry Janyns to redesign St George's Chapel in the Perpendicular Gothic style. Edward was particularly interested in having his own funeral monument in the new chapel, although it was nowhere near ready when he died in April 1483. This was the era of the Wars of the Roses, fought between the Lancastrian and Yorkist royal houses; the previous Lancastrian king, Henry VI, had been murdered in 1471, probably on the orders of the Yorkist Edward IV. Henry's body was moved from Chertsey Abbey in Surrey to St George's Chapel in 1485 and almost immediately miracles began to happen. This led to a cult that centred round Henry's tomb, and it soon became a site of pilgrimage. People suffering from headaches were said to be cured by putting on Henry's hat.

Henry VII took note of this in 1493 when he began to consider where he himself should be buried and he embarked upon an ambitious building project, which involved pulling down part of St George's Chapel and erecting a new Lady Chapel in its place. Work went well until 1498 when a lawsuit determined that Henry VI had wanted to be buried in Westminster Abbey and that his body should be transferred there. A Lady Chapel was duly built for him in the Abbey, although his body was never moved from Windsor. This chapel at Westminster is now known as the Henry VII Chapel, and contains his body instead.

Many succeeding monarchs have also played their part in the evolution of St George's Chapel, which today is a rich and complex building that bears more resemblance to a cathedral than a chapel. It is lavishly decorated with oak carving, as befits a royal chapel dedicated to the highest Order of Chivalry in the country and one of the most important in medieval Europe. There have been many royal weddings here, including

OPPOSITE: The Grand Reception Room is decorated in the style of the French Revival. The Gobelin tapestries on the walls were bought in Paris for George IV.

BELOW: The Garter Ceremony takes place each June, when existing Knights of the Garter watch new Knights being invested with their insignia. The public can watch the procession through the Lower Ward.

that of the Prince of Wales (later Edward VII) to Princess Alexandra on 10 March 1863, and Prince Edward to Sophie Rhys-Jones on 19 June 1999. St George's is also the burial place of ten sovereigns: those medieval enemies, Edward IV and Henry VI, lie on either side of the High Altar, and the bodies of George III, George IV and William IV are in the Royal Vault. The body of Charles I was buried under the choir in a vault that already contained the coffins of Jane Seymour and Henry VIII.

St George's Chapel suffered badly during the Civil War, when many of its ornaments were removed and all the plate was melted down. The castle itself, in common with many other royal residences, was taken over by Parliamentarian forces and the apartments in the Upper Ward were turned into prisons for Royalists. When Charles II regained the throne in 1660 he had much work to do in restoring the many royal residences that had been damaged and sacked by the Parliamentarians. He commissioned new Crown Jewels to replace the lost royal regalia, as well as new plate for the altar in St George's Chapel.

Charles II

Charles wanted a baroque palace whose architecture reflected the importance of the Order of the Garter, so the buildings in the Upper Ward were remodelled at a cost of over £130,000. The new state apartments were created in 1675–8, after which work began on the Royal Chapel and St George's Hall. Antonio Verrio created the painted decorations, which established his career in Britain and led to many other prestigious commissions. Grinling Gibbons also established himself as a woodcarver of genius through his work at Windsor. Charles II was also responsible for buying back the parcels of land within Windsor Great Park that had been sold off during the Civil War, and for planting the Long Walk of elms between 1683–5. His successors, William III and Queen Anne, both contributed to the gardens at Windsor, but the first two Hanoverian kings, George I and George II, had little interest in the castle and turned much of the Upper Ward into grace-and-favour apartments.

George III

George III liked Windsor Castle. Hampton Court conjured up unhappy family memories that he wanted to forget, so he chose Windsor Castle as his main country residence. He also took a fancy to the Queen's Lodge, the small brick house, south of the castle, that Queen Anne had occasionally used as a lodge when stag-hunting. It was too small for him, however, so rebuilding started in 1778, supervised by Sir William Chambers who told the king that the castle could never be made into a comfortable home. Indeed, at the time some of the state apartments were regularly opened to the public and schoolchildren even played within the precincts of the castle.

In June 1790, a small house at Frogmore, to the south of Home Park, was purchased for George's consort, Queen Charlotte. This was followed, two years later, by the acquisition of the estate at Great Frogmore, and the queen began to enlarge and improve the house there, called Frogmore House. In 1841, long after Charlotte's death, the estate at Frogmore was formally linked to Windsor Castle and became an official royal residence. That same year, Queen Victoria's mother, the Duchess of Kent, moved to Frogmore where she spent the rest of her life, dying there on 16 March 1861.

The architect, James Wyatt, remodelled Frogmore House so successfully that he was appointed Surveyor-General in 1796 and commissioned to work on Windsor Castle. The work began in 1800 and was still unfinished in 1811 when George III became incapacitated by porphyria, which was then a mystery illness. We now know that porphyria is a disorder of the blood that poisons the entire nervous

BELOW: The kitchens at Windsor Castle are in the Upper Ward, and were built during the reign of Edward III in the fourteenth century. The original timber roof has survived for six centuries.

system, including the brain, which was why George III was misdiagnosed as being insane. George had already had one attack of the disease in 1788, which resulted in him attacking the Prince of Wales at dinner, on 5 November at Windsor Castle, and trying to smash his head against the wall. Despite hideous so-called cures administered by his doctors, George III had recovered by the spring of 1789. It was a different story in 1811 when, pushed to the limit by grief at the death of his youngest daughter Amelia, he finally became irrevocably ill. He spent the rest of his life in an isolated set of rooms at Windsor Castle, lonely and blind, with the Star of the Order of the Garter pinned to his chest as a nostalgic reminder that he had once been king.

ABOVE: The wooden choir stalls in St George's Chapel date from the fifteenth century. The crests of the members of the Order of the Garter line the walls and their banners hang above them.

Expensive Refurbishments

The Prince of Wales became the Prince Regent, which added further fuel to what was already his burning desire to create some exquisitely palatial royal residences. He became George IV in 1820, and set about transforming St James's Palace, Buckingham Palace and

Windsor Castle into magnificent palaces. In 1823 he moved from Royal Lodge, a *cottage orné*, which he had built in the middle of the Great Park, into the castle itself but, as happened so often with him, found that it could not meet his needs. Parliament pledged £150,000 for the remodelling work, although it eventually cost close to £1 million.

The Round Tower was raised by 9 metres (30 feet), the Long Walk was extended up to the castle and the George IV Gateway was created as the new main entrance. King George IV's Tower and what is now the Cornwall Tower were built, and the exteriors of the buildings in the Upper Ward were given a Gothic appearance. George IV did not care for the royal apartments that his father had occupied in the north range of the Upper Ward, opting instead for the east and south ranges, where a completely new set of rooms was built for him, using a Gothic style for the processional and eating areas and a French style for the drawing rooms and royal apartments. Much of the furniture and other items that George IV had amassed in Carlton House were moved to Windsor Castle: Carlton House was due to be demolished in order to fund the work being carried out at Buckingham Palace. No expense was spared at Windsor, much to the dismay of Parliament who, as usual, had to watch the dizzying costs that were incurred.

Victoria

Queen Victoria adored Windsor Castle, and it became the stage set for many magnificent state visits and family gatherings. However, visits to the castle could be a trial for those who felt the cold, as Victoria enjoyed plenty of fresh air and cool temperatures in the rooms, and expected her guests to like the same. After the queen retired to bed each evening, the men were free to smoke in the billiard room at the end of the north wing; this was so far from the rest of the castle that some guests were unable to find their way back to their rooms through the gloomy corridors (Victoria disliked gaslight and the castle was lit by candles) and had to spend the night on the nearest sofa. Windsor had particular significance for Victoria because her adored husband, Prince Albert, died here on 14 December 1861, and for the rest of her forty years she kept his bedroom, the Blue Room, exactly as he had left it. She was so traumatized and saddened by the experience that she conceived a dislike of blue that lasted for the rest of her life. Victoria created another shrine for Albert in the Albert Memorial Chapel, which was built in the shell of the old Lady Chapel in St George's Chapel. She also created the Royal Mausoleum at Frogmore, where she was buried beside Albert in 1901.

OPPOSITE: St George's Hall was destroyed in the massive fire that swept through Windsor Castle on 20 November 1992. It has been restored and now has the largest hammerbeam roof to have been created since the Middle Ages.

LEFT: The Crimson Drawing Room, built for George IV, was another casualty of the 1992 fire but has now been fully restored. The chimney-piece and carved doors were brought from Carlton House, the London home of George IV, before it was demolished in the 1820s.

HAMPTON COURT PALACE

The early history of Hampton Court Palace is a moral tale that warns against the perils of greed, hubris and of reaching an exalted position that attracts envy. Although it is now one of the great royal palaces in Britain, if not the world, Hampton Court was originally the home of a commoner, Thomas Wolsey, whose star shone very brightly in the Tudor firmament before it was snuffed out by a situation he was powerless to control.

Wolsey

Born in the early 1470s, Wolsey was the son of an Ipswich butcher but his ambitions soon took him into the church, where he climbed up the ecclesiastical greasy pole in record time. Having been chaplain to Henry VII, he was in a good position to pursue his ambitions when Henry's son, Henry VIII, succeeded to the throne in 1509. Wolsey quickly attained a series of bishoprics, which offered him great financial rewards as well as considerable prestige. He became Lord Chancellor and Cardinal in 1515, and immediately set about creating a home that would reflect his tremendous importance and wealth.

Wolsey had acquired the lease on Hampton Court in 1514, when it was still a relatively modest country house. It was not long before the place became a hub of activity, swarming with builders, carpenters and masons. Wolsey wanted a home in which he could entertain on a lavish scale, with a suite of apartments that would be suitable for Henry VIII, his wife Katherine of Aragon and their daughter Princess Mary. Forty of Wolsey's guest suites were built around Base Court and each one offered an outer and an inner room, plus a lavatory (known at the time as a garderobe). The royal apartments were in what is now part of the Georgian Rooms.

There was no doubt that Wolsey was in the ascendant as one of the most powerful men in the kingdom. However, nemesis eventually arrived in the guise of Anne Boleyn and what was known as the King's Great Matter. Henry's wife, Katherine, had failed to produce a living male heir to the throne, which was a source of great concern. Henry needed to find a solution and he did not have to look far. He was obsessed with Anne Boleyn, one of Katherine's ladies-in-waiting and whose beauty, youth and apparent fertility were in marked contrast to the now faded charms of his wife. It was becoming increasingly obvious that he must divorce Katherine and marry Anne, and it fell to Wolsey to arrange this with the Pope. The Pope, however, refused to countenance such a step, and the problem was compounded further by difficulties within Europe and by the enmity that Anne felt towards Wolsey. After further delays, over which he had no control, Wolsey's fate was sealed. Besides this, he had become far too powerful and rich for Henry's liking: Wolsey's wealth alone amounted to one-third of the ordinary revenues of the Crown. He was arrested in October 1529 and then pardoned, but was arrested again the following year and died on his way to the Tower of London.

Henry VIII

In the meantime, Hampton Court had already changed hands when Henry forced Wolsey to surrender it in 1528. This was, after all, a period in history when monarchs had absolute power, and Henry had so much working in his favour. He was still a relatively young man who had good cause to be optimistic when he took over the

ownership of Hampton Court and embarked on a fresh round of building work. He had plenty of money as his exchequer had been greatly increased by the spoils from the dissolution of the monasteries in 1536, which followed England's rebuttal of Catholicism and the beginning of the English Reformation. Hampton Court became a most splendid royal palace, with running water (the height of innovative luxury at the time), formal gardens, massive kitchens that can still be seen today, a magnificent Chapel Royal (Henry always prided himself on his devout nature, even though history presents his character in a less sanctified light) and luxurious state and private apartments that were remodelled again and again according to his whims.

The Elizabethan Court

Henry owned more than sixty houses and considered Hampton Court to be his fourth favourite after Whitehall Palace, Greenwich Palace and Windsor Castle. There was great joy at Hampton Court when Henry's only surviving and legitimate male heir, Prince Edward (later Edward VI), was born on 12 October 1537, followed by grief when his wife, Jane Seymour, died twelve days later; and optimism when he married his sixth wife, Katherine Parr, in the Holyday Closet above the Chapel Royal on 12 July 1543. After his death in 1547, Henry's Tudor heirs continued to visit Hampton Court but never carried out much building work. Elizabeth I almost died from smallpox at Hampton Court in 1562, which made her reluctant to go near it again for some time, but eventually the Elizabethan court would celebrate Easter, Whitsun and some Christmases here. Plays were staged with elaborate preparation in the Great Hall, even to the extent of providing artificial snow. Nevertheless, Elizabeth always thought that the palace was unhealthy and she mainly used it for important occasions when it was necessary to impress visiting dignitaries. Elizabeth was intolerant of certain smells, including those from the privy kitchen beneath her apartments. The offending kitchen was moved to another part of the palace in 1567. The gardens, however, pleased her and she enjoyed working in them. When potatoes and tobacco plants were discovered in the New World, they were imported and planted at Hampton Court.

The Civil War

When Elizabeth died on 24 March 1603, her successor was James I, who had been James VI of Scotland. He liked Hampton Court because he enjoyed hunting in the park. His son, Charles I, spent his honeymoon here in the summer of 1625 with his French bride, Henrietta Maria. Later on in his reign, Charles had less happy memories of the place as he was imprisoned here in 1647, during the Civil War. It was at this point in its history that Hampton Court fell into the possession of Parliamentary forces, who systematically stripped it of most of its treasures and sold them. The palace itself was sold to an Edmund Backwall in 1652, but was bought back for Oliver Cromwell after he became Lord Protector in 1653.

After the Restoration of the monarchy in 1660, Hampton Court once again became a royal palace, although it was never a favourite of Charles II. It was, however, the perfect place for him to store important paintings during the Great Fire of London in 1666. During this time, Charles II was also busy retrieving lost royal treasures: Cromwell's widow surrendered seventeen cartloads of royal belongings.

A Second Renaissance

Hampton Court enjoyed a second renaissance when William III and Mary II succeeded to the throne in 1689. Although the new king and queen liked both the palace and its grounds (clean air for the asthmatic William), they found the buildings antiquated and uncomfortable. Consequently, Sir Christopher Wren was asked to pull down almost the entire Tudor palace, with the exception of the Great Hall, and to rebuild it in a modern style reminiscent of the magnificent Palace of Versailles. Despite allocating vast sums to the rebuilding work, William and Mary's budget failed to run to such drastic structural changes and they had to compromise: the old Tudor lodgings on the south and east sides of the palace were demolished and replaced with the royal couple's new apartments. William and Mary were impatient owners and wanted instant results, which translated into rushed and poor building work. This had tragic results in December 1689 when, only seven months after work had started, a large section of the south range collapsed, killing two workmen and injuring eleven others. There was a further setback in December 1694 when Mary died of smallpox, and all building work was suspended until 1698. When work finally resumed, it was conducted by Wren's deputy as Wren himself had submitted an estimate that was considered to be too expensive – the Nine Years War against France had just ended and the budget was tight. Sadly, William had little time to enjoy his palace as he died in 1702, after breaking his collarbone when he fell from his horse while riding near Hampton Court. The horse had tripped over a molehill and when William, never a popular king, died, the English Jacobites, who had so opposed his reign, invented the toast: 'To the little gentleman in black velvet' – in other words, to the mole whose hill had caused William's death.

OPPOSITE: The vast complex of the Tudor Kitchens is the engine room of the palace, and was capable of feeding Henry VIII's household of 1200 people in only two sittings.

BELOW: Queen Victoria opened Hampton Court to the public in 1838 and, in an age where travel was becoming easier, it soon became a popular tourist destination. By 1897, over eleven million people had visited the palace.

Refurbishment of the Chapel Royal

Queen Anne inherited the throne and, with it, Hampton Court. However, the Queen's Apartments were still being built so she had to stay in the King's Apartments. She enjoyed hunting but her frail health meant she had to follow the hounds in a cart along a specially constructed track. One of her greatest legacies was the refurbishment of the Chapel Royal, executed by Sir Christopher Wren. All that remains of the Tudor chapel is the intricate gilded ceiling, installed by Henry VIII in 1535–6. The Royal Pew, which looks down on the chapel from the gallery above, was constructed for Queen Anne, necessitating rudimentary divisions across the beautiful old ceiling. It is amusing to note that unsympathetic changes to ancient buildings have been carried out down the centuries, sometimes by the most celebrated names: architectural vandalism is nothing new.

The Hanoverian Dynasty

When George I came to Britain from Hanover after attaining the throne in 1714, he could not speak English and preferred to stay out of the limelight. However, his son and daughter-in-law, the Prince and Princess of Wales (later George II and Queen Caroline), enjoyed court life and spent a great deal of time at Hampton Court. They used the Queen's Apartments from the summer of 1716 onwards.

During the Hanoverian dynasty there was invariably trouble between father and eldest son, and this duly flared up between George I and the Prince of Wales. George was jealous of his son's success and popularity, and finally reacted to this by banning the Prince from court in 1717. George I held a full court at Hampton Court in 1718, before patching up the argument with his son and once again retreating into a more private life. When George I died in 1727, the new George II and Queen Caroline were more than happy to continue renovating Hampton Court. The rooms known today as the Cumberland Rooms were built in 1732 for their second son, the Duke of Cumberland, and were designed by William Kent. As it turned out, they were the last rooms to be built at Hampton Court for a member of the royal family.

The full English court visited Hampton Court for the last time in 1737, when Caroline died on 20 November of that year. It was the end of Hampton Court's role as a working royal palace, entertaining a full court. After George II died in 1760, his grandson, George III, made it plain that he had no interest in Hampton Court. Apparently, this was because George II had once boxed his ears in the state apartments. A resident staff of forty, including the landscape gardener, 'Capability' Brown, looked after the palace but its furniture and other treasures were gradually transferred to other royal palaces. Many of the apartments were assigned, rent-free, to people who had given great service to king or country, and were known as grace-and-favour apartments. This system operated until the 1970s, although many people who help to run Hampton Court still live here.

Fire and Restoration

Hampton Court might have fallen out of royal favour but it was still of great interest to architects and historians. Restoration was

BELOW: The Privy Garden was the private garden of the reigning monarch. In the 1990s it was restored to its original, 1702, appearance when it was planted for William III.

carried out between 1838 and 1851, with several areas of the palace stripped of their 'improvements' and restored to their original Tudor appearance. Another phase of restoration work took place between 1875 and 1900, again concentrating on the Tudor areas of the palace. The palace was opened to the public in 1838, but this was not the first time as in the sixteenth century Elizabeth I had also allowed paying visitors to view some areas of the palace.

On 31 March 1986, fire broke out in one of the grace-and-favour apartments on the third floor of the wing containing the King's Apartments. Timber and molten lead fell into the apartments below, causing immense damage to the Cartoon Gallery and King's Privy Chamber. It took six years to repair them, but it was an opportunity to restore them to their original appearance. Whenever possible, this was done using traditional techniques and materials that would have been familiar to Sir Christopher Wren, the chief architect at the time.

Hampton Court Today

Hampton Court now resembles a small city with its beautifully arranged courtyards, ancient courts whose flagstones show the outlines of previous buildings that stood there and its many rooms and staircases. The palace itself covers almost 3 hectares (7 acres) of land, with a further 24 hectares (60 acres) of garden. Each section of the palace has its own distinct atmosphere, from the relatively plain designs of the rooms in Henry VIII's State Apartments to the cosy intimacy of the Queen's Private Apartments, built for Mary II who died before she was able to enjoy them. Many of the ceilings in the palace apartments are ornate and very beautiful, whether they are ribbed Tudor ceilings, baroque plasterwork or adorned with paintings, such as those in the Queen's State Apartments. When the Duke of Württemberg visited the palace in 1590, he wrote in his diary: 'Now this is the most splendid and most magnificent royal palace of any that may be found in England, or indeed in any other Kingdom.' This is an assertion still worthy of consideration today.

ABOVE: The King's Privy Chamber was the most important ceremonial room in the palace. William III would sit under the throne canopy during his audiences with members of the court.

SANDRINGHAM HOUSE

Sandringham House has always been more of a private royal home than a palace. Since the 1870s, it has offered four generations of the royal family a chance to retreat from the heavy demands of state and protocol into their own more tranquil and private world. As far as George V was concerned, Sandringham was 'the place I love better than anywhere else in the world'. He described it as 'dear old Sandringham', and took great comfort from its informal atmosphere.

A Family Home

The Sandringham Estate was originally acquired by the Prince of Wales, later Edward VII, from the Hon. Charles Spencer Cowper in 1862. When the Prince first saw it, Sandringham House was a Georgian building that, while perfectly pleasant, was not nearly large enough for his needs. After his marriage to the Danish Princess Alexandra, in 1863, it was obvious that Sandringham would need to be a family home, and it was duly enlarged between 1869 and 1870 in the style of a comfortable country house. Sandringham was never intended to be a palace, so there was no need for any rooms for state functions. Besides, when foreign royalty came to stay, they were usually relatives of either the Prince or Princess (Queen Victoria, whose children married into several foreign royal families, was known as 'the grandmother of Europe'), so their visits could be conducted in a very relaxed fashion. State visits were for London, family visits for Sandringham. After a major fire in 1891, the house was extended once again and an east wing was built. The outward appearance of this, in red brick and brown carstone, is in marked contrast to the red brick and yellow stone of the rest of the house.

The Social Prince

When the Prince of Wales bought Sandringham, he was in sore need of something to occupy his time and energy. His father, Prince Albert, had died unexpectedly the year before, in 1861, and his mother, Queen Victoria, had immersed herself in widowhood and showed little sign of ever emerging from it. Nevertheless, the grieving queen kept a firm grip on her constitutional duties and was profoundly reluctant to allow her eldest son to help her in any way. She refused to let him have anything to do with state papers, as she believed that he would be indiscreet about them, so this left him with very little to occupy his time. Barred from any involvement with the official side of monarchy, the Prince of Wales took over the social side instead. His mother had effectively disappeared from public view, leaving a huge gap that needed to be filled, and it was important to maintain a strong presence among the British people. Indeed, Queen Victoria's self-imposed retreat from the public eye eventually stirred up republican sympathies in some of her subjects. Together, the newly married Prince and Princess of Wales embarked on the hectic duties of constitutional monarchy: opening bridges, planting trees and meeting the people. They also became the pivot around which the highest echelons of fashionable Victorian society revolved.

ABOVE: *The lakes at Sandringham were created for Prince Edward and Princess Alexandra by Sir William Broderick Thomas, who also landscaped the gardens.*

A Country Retreat

The Prince and Princess of Wales had two homes: Sandringham in Norfolk and Marlborough House in Pall Mall, London. Although the Prince's life in London attracted a good deal of high-minded Victorian criticism and barely suppressed whispers of scandal (he was never short of mistresses), his visits to Sandringham received much less censure. Here, he could behave like a typical hunting-shooting-fishing member of the nineteenth-century aristocracy, visiting his tenants, throwing country house parties for his many friends and generally setting a good example to the locals. After the death of Queen Victoria on 22 January 1901, the royal couple became King Edward VII and Queen Alexandra, and Sandringham became an even more welcome retreat from the rigours of duty and protocol.

Edward VII and his cronies spent a good deal of time in the billiard room at Sandringham, where one can imagine them all smoking, drinking and exchanging risqué stories of female conquests. Queen Alexandra's province was the elegant, large drawing room, where she did a great deal of entertaining. This room was also much loved by her daughter-in-law, Queen Mary, who collected the jade and crystal that is on display there.

George V

After Edward died, on 6 May 1910, the Sandringham estate passed to his only surviving son and heir, George V. Queen Alexandra moved back to Marlborough House, which had been her home while she was Princess of Wales, but she still visited Sandringham and died there on 20 November 1925.

Like his father, George V dearly loved shooting at Sandringham, using cartridges stamped with a tiny red crown. Game birds were plentiful, which was just as well as 10,000 of them were once killed during a four-day shoot. Despite regularly being responsible for such carnage, George V considered himself to be a great animal lover and was once moved to tears on finding a dead bird in the garden at

PAGE 25: The Small Drawing Room has an intimate atmosphere. The walls are hung with English silk and the seat covers of the Sheraton-style armchairs were stitched by Queen Mary in 1935.

LEFT: Gardening has always been a favourite hobby of members of the royal family. Princess Alexandra had a powerful influence on the landscaping of the grounds at Sandringham. She wanted the new, naturalistic style being pioneered by William Robinson rather than the fussy bedding-out schemes of the Victorians.

Windsor. He had a pet parrot, called Charlotte, who travelled with him whenever possible, and at Sandringham she would accompany him in to breakfast perched on his finger; Charlotte would then trample all over the table, causing utter havoc. George V was also fond of big game hunting, and in 1928 he created his own museum of trophies in rooms attached to the stable block.

George V and Queen Mary adored Sandringham, living in the modest York Cottage in the grounds of the estate rather than in the 'big house', and all their children, with the exception of the Prince of Wales (later Edward VIII), were born on the estate. The Prince of Wales once told Harold Nicolson, the MP and diarist, 'Until you have seen York Cottage you will never understand my father.' Having seen it, Nicolson wrote, 'There is nothing to differentiate the cottage from any of the villas at Surbiton... The King's and Queen's baths had lids that shut down so that when not in use they could be used as tables.'

George V died peacefully at Sandringham on 20 January 1936, a year that was to have momentous consequences for Britain, because it saw three kings on the throne: George V, Edward VIII and George VI. The death of George V is famous as his doctor, Lord Dawson of Penn, hastened it with an injection of morphine so that it could be announced in the morning papers and also relieve the strain on the royal family, who were waiting for the king to slip from a coma into death.

Abdication and the Making of a Relaxed Home
Edward VIII had little time or affection for Sandringham during his short reign. He also abominated one of the traditions of the house, which had been introduced by his grandfather, Edward VII, of keeping the clocks half an hour fast ('Sandringham time') in order to have as much daylight as possible for shooting. After his abdication, the newly styled Duke of Windsor sold Sandringham to his successor and brother, George VI, who loved the place. He was born here on 14 December 1895, the anniversary of Prince Albert's death, and was named after him. He was the second son of George V and therefore had never imagined taking over the duties of his older brother, Edward VIII.

Public duties were arduous and nerve-racking for George VI, who was a shy man, but he took great solace from Sandringham and also from his wife, Queen Elizabeth, and their happy family life with their daughters, the Princesses Elizabeth and Margaret. Sandringham in the 1940s and 1950s felt like a very different place from the one in which George VI had grown up. The Countess of Airlie had been lady-in-waiting to Queen Mary, and wrote of George VI's tenure: 'There was no denying that the atmosphere of Sandringham was very much more friendly than in the old days, more like that of any home. One senses far more the setting of ordinary family life in this generation than in the last.' She even noted that a table covered with jigsaw puzzles stood in the entrance hall.

George VI died at his beloved Sandringham on 6 February 1952 while his daughter, Princess Elizabeth, was visiting Kenya with her husband, the Duke of Edinburgh. Since then, the Queen and her family have spent each Christmas at Sandringham, staying here until after the February anniversary of her father's death and of her succession to the throne.

Modern Connections
On 1 July 1961, Lady Diana Spencer was born at Park House, on the Sandringham Estate, and grew up here. In later life, she admitted that her roots were in Norfolk. Even before she married, Diana already had royal connections: her grandfather, the 4th Lord Fermoy, had leased Park House from George V, and her grandmother became a lady-in-waiting to the Queen Mother in 1955. Her father, who was then Lord Althorp but who later became Earl Spencer, had been an equerry to George VI in 1950–52 and had subsequently worked in the household of Elizabeth II in 1952–54. In 1981, the

world was overtaken by 'Diana-mania' when she married Prince Charles; she was the first English bride of an heir to the British throne since James II married Lady Anne Hyde in 1659. Charles and Diana were divorced in 1996 and another outbreak of 'Diana-mania' swept the world, this time in much sadder circumstances, when she was killed in a car crash in Paris on 31 August 1997.

Today, the Sandringham Estate is a thriving commercial concern run by a land agent on the Queen's behalf. In addition to farming, the land is used for forestry, two stud farms and a 267-hectare (660-acre) country park, which is open to the public throughout the year. Yet Sandringham has not lost its original purpose of offering a safe haven to members of the royal family when they want to indulge their love of the countryside and a simpler way of life away from the public and media.

BELOW: The Walled Garden is one of the many small gardens within the grounds of the Sandringham Estate. Cutbacks in the number of staff since the 1930s have inevitably led to changes to some of these gardens in order to reduce the amount of maintenance they need.

THE ROYAL PAVILION

Of all the people that have made up the British royal family in the past thousand years, few have provoked more criticism and dislike than the Prince Regent, who became George IV in 1820. He was notorious in his day for his extravagance, licentiousness, self-indulgence and wild flights of fancy. Contemporary cartoonists, such as James Gilray and George Cruikshank, delighted in producing scabrous and vicious comments on his musicianship, love life, portly figure, clothes, spending habits and anything else that they felt was fair game. William Thackeray, writing about him in *The Four Georges*, said: 'I try to take him to pieces, and find silk stockings, padding, stays, a coat with frogs and a fur collar, and star and blue ribbon, a pocket-handkerchief prodigiously scented, one of Truefitt's best nutty-brown wigs reeking with oil, a set of teeth and a huge black stock, underwaistcoats, more underwaistcoats, and then nothing.'

What Thackeray fails to mention is the magnificent cultural legacy that George IV left behind. His Regency period saw a host of artistic achievements, one of the greatest of which was undoubtedly his own Royal Pavilion in Brighton. This astonishing phantasmagoria of domes, minarets and tented roofs was the pet project of the then Prince of Wales for almost twenty years, and a showcase for the talents of the architects Henry Holland and John Nash. The interior of the Pavilion was breathtaking in its extravagance and decoration, even in an era noted for its lavish way of life.

Extravagance and Debt

In the 1780s, Brighthelmstone, as Brighton was then known, was highly fashionable and was said by the *Morning Herald* to be 'the Paris of its day'. Sea bathing was all the rage, and the town enjoyed royal patronage from the Duke of Cumberland, brother of George III. When the Prince of Wales visited his uncle there in 1783 he was captivated, and took Grove House, where the Music Room of the Pavilion now stands, for the season the following year. Already, at the age of 22, the Prince of Wales was £250,000 in debt, having spent a fortune on renovating Carlton House in London. He was unable to budget or control his spending, nor did he see why he should. His father, George III, refused to help unless the Prince of Wales gave a full account of all his debts but this was not an acceptable proposal for the prince. Work stopped on Carlton House and he announced that he had decided to live like a private gentleman in Brighton. He leased a farmhouse, called Brighton House, between the Castle Inn and Grove House.

Marine Pavilion

The prince loved renovating houses and it was not long before Henry Holland, the architect who had worked on Carlton House, was summoned to Brighton. By 1788 Brighton House was known as the Marine Pavilion and had undergone the first of many transformations; a rotunda, bow windows and an oriental dome were added, although most of the exterior was still quite plain. The prince's private life had also undergone a transformation, as he had secretly married Maria Fitzherbert, a young Catholic widow, in 1785. This was in direct contravention to the Royal Marriages Act of 1772, designed to prevent members of the royal family making unsuitable or scandalous marriages: the marriage of a Protestant heir to the British throne to a Catholic widow came under

OPPOSITE: *The King's Apartment is typical of the overblown richness of the Prince's retreat. Between 1815 and 1822 John Nash created the Chinese-style interior as well as the Indian exterior of the Pavilion.*

BELOW: *The Royal Pavilion is in the centre of the city, and a stone's throw from the sea, the real reason the prince wanted his fabulous experiment of living like a private gentleman in Brighton.*

both categories, and was therefore invalid. As it turned out, Mrs Fitzherbert was a good influence on the prince, curbing many of his excesses while making him happy. The couple were generous and popular patrons of Brighton.

An Unhappy Marriage

By the early 1790s, the marriage was foundering. The prince had been enticed away from his practical, eminently sensible wife by the wily Lady Jersey, a member of the court, and was once again heavily in debt. Faced with little option, he made a deal with Parliament and agreed to an arranged marriage with his first cousin, Caroline of Brunswick, in return for Parliament paying off his debts. Almost as soon as it began, in 1795, it was an unhappy marriage, with each party being profoundly disappointed by the unprepossessing appearance of the other, although not before Princess Caroline had conceived a child. This seems nothing short of a miracle as the prince is alleged to have spent the wedding night drunk, laid out cold on the floor and with his head in the bedroom fireplace; by the next day he had sexually washed his hands of his new wife. Incidentally, Caroline did not hold with washing and prided herself on her short *toilettes*, very rarely changing her underclothes. This was anathema to the prince, who was obsessed with his clothes and spent hours each day on his own *toilette*.

The estranged couple continued to keep up appearances in public, as the prospect of a royal divorce was unthinkable. Their private life, however, was in a state of war, a situation not helped by the constant presence of Lady Jersey, who was Caroline's lady-in-waiting as well as the prince's mistress. Further disappointment arrived when Caroline's baby was born a girl. By 1800, his relationship with Lady Jersey over and his marriage in shreds, the prince successfully persuaded Mrs Fitzherbert to return to him. She played hard to get and only conceded after she had secured a Papal confirmation of the canonical validity of her marriage to the prince. All was well once more, and Mrs Fitzherbert became a good and restraining influence on him. They lived together very happily for the next eight years.

Enlargements and Extensions

Brighton, in the meantime, had become a mini court, and Henry Holland was asked to extend and alter the Pavilion. It was at this point that the Chinese style, which is so pronounced at the Pavilion, began to appear. Chinoiserie, a European decorative art form that was influenced by China, and had been all the rage in the second half of the eighteenth century, was no longer de rigueur in domestic interiors of fashionable houses. Despite this, the prince sparked a revival.

In 1812, James Wyatt, the Crown's Surveyor-General, was commissioned to enlarge the Pavilion at an estimated cost of £100,000. However, he died in 1813 and John Nash was asked to take over. Nash was already an accomplished architect, used to working for royalty and the aristocracy. He had rebuilt Royal Lodge in Windsor Park in 1813 as a *cottage orné*, and was working on rooms at Carlton House at the time of the commission. Some of Nash's work on the Pavilion was revolutionary. The Great Dome over the Saloon, for example, was built in 1818 and was a feat of engineering; the prince even made a special journey from London to see it erected. The original structure was not strong enough to support the weight of the dome, so Nash built a huge iron cage, on which the dome could rest, around the exterior walls. In 1819 the Pavilion received further exterior adornments, with minarets, small domes and columns made of Bath stone. Unfortunately, the ironwork used for the cages and the cores in the small minarets eventually started to rust and expand, causing many problems.

Although there were more plans for building at the southwest of the pavilion, Nash's work was almost over by the end of 1820. There was a brief rift between Nash and the prince, who was by now King George IV, when the mastic stucco on the roofs began to let in water, which caused much damage over the years. The tent roofs above the Music and Banqueting Rooms were re-covered in copper in 1827.

OPPOSITE: The Great Kitchen was nothing short of a marvel when it was first built. Although it was designed as a highly efficient kitchen that would be able to cope with George IV's lavish style of entertaining, it was still decorated in the style of the Pavilion, with copper palm trees topping the cast-iron columns.

RIGHT: The Banqueting Room was created by John Nash between 1817 and 1820. The central gasolier is so heavy that in 1834 William IV had it removed for fear it would fall on someone; it was reinstalled in 1842 on the orders of Queen Victoria. This was the first room in Brighton to be illuminated and heated by gas, and both the Prince Regent and John Nash were present when this momentous event took place.

William IV

As he became older, George IV's health declined. He was plagued by dropsy and gout, neither condition helped by his considerable size and his enthusiasm for wine. He was also a victim of the success that he had made of Brighton, and became unnerved by the inquisitive crowds that plagued him there; his last visit was in 1827. Ever the enthusiastic renovator, however, he was not idle in London and was also busy refurbishing Windsor Castle and Buckingham Palace. When George IV died in 1830, Brighton collectively held its breath. Although his brother had had his own apartment within the Pavilion when he was Duke of Clarence, would he still patronize it now that he was king? Thankfully, yes, and Brighton gave a triumphal welcome to William IV and Queen Adelaide. More building work ensued, creating rooms for visitors and servants, with John Nash now acting as advisor while the work was carried out by the architect Joseph Good. William had neither the taste nor the imagination of George IV, believing that houses should be as plain as possible, but he enjoyed his visits to the Pavilion and left the decorations intact.

The Pavilion is Sold

His successor, Queen Victoria, did not spend much time at the Pavilion, preferring to remove much of its contents to Buckingham Palace. Besides, it was too vivid a reminder of those she thought of as her 'wicked uncles'. In 1846, it was announced that the Pavilion was to be sold in order to pay for the extensions to Buckingham Palace. The contents were systematically removed to other royal palaces. Despite a Parliamentary proposal that the Pavilion be demolished and the land used without restriction, the town of Brighton eventually bought it in 1849. The Pavilion was gradually restored to its former splendour, with most of the decorations returned by Queen Victoria in 1863. It went through a curious period in the First World War when it was used as a military hospital, but Queen Mary, the grand-niece of George IV, took an active interest in its welfare from 1912 onwards. The Pavilion again went into a decline during the Second World War, after which there was once more talk of demolition. Since then, there has been increasing interest in the splendours of the Pavilion, and painstaking restoration work has continued on this rich, architectural fantasia, a fitting memorial to one of Britain's most vivid and interesting monarchs.

OSBORNE HOUSE

Queen Victoria and her husband, Prince Albert, bought Osborne House on the Isle of Wight in October 1844. It seemed the perfect choice for the private home that they were searching for, away from the rigours of court life. Queen Victoria, who was always prone to impulses prompted by nostalgia, was interested in buying a house on the Isle of Wight because she had enjoyed two summer holidays there as a young girl. The Royal Pavilion at Brighton had been mooted as a prospective home, but the Queen dismissed it because she did not like the building and also because Brighton had become such a busy tourist destination that it offered little chance of seclusion.

Osborne House and its setting immediately entranced Victoria and Albert. It was obvious that the three-storey Georgian house was far too small for their needs, but pulling it down and building something larger easily remedied that. What really captivated them were the views of the Solent, which reminded Albert of the Bay of Naples. This was his inspiration for the Italian Renaissance style of the new house and gardens, and work began almost at once.

The Gardens

The architect was Thomas Cubitt, already at the height of his success. His huge team of workmen ensured that the original building was demolished and replaced by the new Osborne House in as short a time as possible. The gardens were landscaped in suitably Italianate style by Prince Albert in collaboration with Ludwig Grüner, with Albert directing the planting of large specimen trees from his vantage point in one of Osborne's towers. Albert was so caught up in the excitement of creating a private home that he happily planted many of the smaller trees and shrubs himself.

The Swiss Cottage

Another feature in the grounds is the Swiss Cottage, which, as its name implies, was dismantled and brought piece by piece from Switzerland to Osborne, where it was reassembled. It was Victoria's gift to her children on her birthday in 1854, and was where they were encouraged to learn to garden. Each child was given a rectangular plot in which to grow fruit, vegetables and flowers. They would then sell their crops to their father, to give them a secure grounding in simple economics. The children also learnt to cook in the Swiss Cottage, as it had a fully equipped kitchen. There is something very charming about this desire to keep the children's feet on the ground as, even then, it must have been self-evident that they would all marry into the great European families.

Domestic Idyll

Osborne House was a real home to the royal family. It meant so much to them that even the royal yacht was called *Osborne*. They stayed here for four lengthy periods each year: in spring; for Victoria's birthday in May; in July and August, when they celebrated Albert's birthday; and just before Christmas. They allowed photographers and painters to capture incidents from their family life in the grounds and in the house, partly for their own enjoyment and partly as a form of propaganda to the nation, to show what a happy, devoted family they were. Many thousands of prints of the royal family were sold

to the public, and Victoria truly believed that 'no Sovereign was ever more loved than I am (I am bold enough to say)'.

Although Osborne was a beloved family home, it was also the home of a queen and her consort, as the lavish interior decorations show. There are also many reminders of Victoria's dynastic links with the other European royal families: the Billiard Room houses a massive porcelain vase, which was a gift from a Russian Tsar. The grandeur of the Billiard Room, Queen's Dining Room and the Drawing Room on the ground floor forms a marked contrast with the much more homely and unassuming décor of the royal apartments on the first floor. These rooms, which include the Prince's Dressing Room, the Queen's Sitting Room, the Queen's Bedroom and the children's nurseries, were intended for private, domestic use, and were therefore as comfortable as possible. Victoria and Albert wanted to bring up their children in as natural and loving an environment as their situation allowed, so the young princes and princesses often visited their parents' bedrooms; this was not the sort of Victorian upper-class family in which parents and children only met once a day for a short period of stilted conversation.

Osbourne in Mourning

Sadly, this domestic idyll ended at Windsor Castle on 14 December 1861, when Albert died, at the age of 42, from typhoid. Victoria famously went into impenetrable mourning and retreated to Windsor and Osborne with her memories. The private royal apartments were effectively sealed in a time capsule, with everything preserved as it had been when Albert was alive. The domestic routine also continued as though Albert were still alive, even to the extent of his shaving things and clothes being laid out for him each day. When she took decisions, Victoria tried to do whatever she believed her sainted Albert would have done in the same circumstances. She revered him to such an extent that the poor man was unfairly considered to be even more of a bore in death than he had been in life. Such deep, intractable mourning, with its inevitable retreat from her people, almost caused Victoria to lose the throne as it sparked off profound republican sentiments in many corners of her realm. Victoria dedicated herself to erecting monuments to Albert's memory at every opportunity but, apart from that, she chose to stay out of the public gaze for ten years. She described herself as 'a poor weak woman shattered by grief and anxiety'.

Empress of India

It took years for Victoria to return fully to public life, a process that she carried out by degrees. One of the greatest incentives is celebrated at Osborne, in the opulent Durbar Room. In 1876, Victoria was declared Empress of India, which at the time was one of Britain's most glittering colonial possessions. The Durbar Room was built for state functions, and the wing that contains it was added to Osborne House between 1890 and 1891. The room's name is an Anglicized version of the Hindi word *darbar*, which means 'court'. Bhai Ram Singh decorated the Durbar Room in an elaborate and intricate style, with a carpet from Agra. It now contains the gifts Queen Victoria received on her Golden and Diamond Jubilees, in 1887 and 1897 respectively. These include engraved silver and copper vases, Indian armour and even a model of an Indian palace.

Victoria's Death

Queen Victoria died at Osborne House on 22 January 1901, with two generations of her family gathered around her. Although Victoria had adored it, Osborne held few charms for her children. Victoria's will left strict instructions that the house should stay in the family, but no one wanted it and so King Edward VII presented it to the nation. The public was allowed to visit the state apartments, but the private apartments were closed and the rest of the house was used as a Royal Naval College and also as a convalescent home for officers from the army and navy. Today, Osborne House has been extensively refurbished to look as it did in Queen Victoria's time, and recaptures the feel of the home that she loved so dearly for nearly sixty years.

OPPOSITE: The Upper Landing leads to Victoria and Albert's private rooms. The fresco was painted by William Dyce in 1847 and is entitled 'Neptune resigning the Empire of the Seas to Britannia'.

ABOVE: A copy of Franz Winterhalter's famous portrait of Victoria, Albert and their children hangs in the Queen's Dining Room.

HEVER CASTLE

During its eight-hundred-year history, Hever Castle has belonged to two of the most powerful families in Britain. During the sixteenth century, Hever was home to the Bullen family, most of whose members were busily pulling strings and climbing the social ladder at Henry VIII's court. In the early twentieth century, Hever became the domain of William Waldorf Astor, the American multi-millionaire, who transformed it from a near ruin to the picturesque castle that we know today, surrounded by gardens, a lake and a Tudor village.

A Rise to Power

The oldest parts of Hever are the gatehouse, outer walls and moat; the De Hever family, who also gave their name to their new home, built these in 1270. When Sir Geoffrey Bullen, Lord Mayor of London, acquired the castle around 1460, he built a house within the outer walls. The Bullens prospered; Sir Geoffrey's grandson, Sir Thomas, was an ambitious courtier who had the ear of Henry VIII. This was partly due to Thomas's marriage to Elizabeth Howard, the daughter of the 2nd Duke of Norfolk. Having achieved a powerful position within the court, Thomas was anxious to consolidate it and build on it at every opportunity; he pushed forward his three surviving children, Mary, George and Anne, to ensure that they were always at the centre of royal attention.

Anne Boleyn

When she was about thirteen, Anne was sent to France in the retinue of Princess Mary, the sister of Henry VIII, who was marrying King Louis XII. At that time, the French court was the most sophisticated and elegant in Europe and Anne blossomed there. It was during this period that she changed her surname from Bullen to the more euphonious Boleyn. In 1522 Anne returned to England to find it almost unbearably dull and dreary. She was appointed lady-in-waiting to Katherine of Aragon, thereby triggering the start of one of English history's most famous and momentous phases. Not only was it a powerful love story, it also heralded the end of the Pope's influence over England and the beginning of the Church of England, presided over by the reigning monarch.

Although Henry dearly loved Katherine, he was profoundly disappointed by what he saw as her failure to provide him with an heir. Despite six pregnancies, only one child survived infancy and she was a girl, Princess Mary. The previous century had been a very turbulent, war-torn period of English history and Henry was uncomfortably aware that several people had a better claim to the throne than he. He wanted a trouble-free reign in which any rivals to the crown could be swiftly dealt with, and in which an easy succession was assured. By the time Anne came to Henry's notice in the mid 1520s, it was increasingly obvious that Katherine's childbearing days were over. It was time for Henry to find another wife, and Anne seemed an excellent choice. Firstly, Henry had to divorce Katherine, which, as they were both Roman Catholics, was unthinkable because the Pope forbade it. Henry overruled all objections to his divorce, however, announcing that his marriage to Katherine was illegal and incestuous because she had previously been married to his elder brother, Arthur, before his death in 1502. Thomas Cranmer, Archbishop of Canterbury, annulled the marriage on 23 May 1533, although Henry and Anne had already married in secret in January of that year.

The Bullen family was already elevated, thanks to Henry's passion for Anne, but their star rose even higher once Anne was crowned Queen Consort on 1 June 1533. They now had tremendous power and influence, but it did not last. In what must have felt like a ghastly re-enactment of Henry's first marriage, Anne was unable to produce a surviving male heir. Once again, the only living child was a girl, Princess Elizabeth.

At first saddened, Henry soon became furiously angry. He convinced himself that the

OPPOSITE: Henry VIII always travelled with his own locks, one of which can be seen on a door in the Dining Hall.

BELOW: The Dining Hall is one of the rooms that was restored by William Astor between 1903 and 1906.

entire problem lay with Anne, and that the solution therefore lay in her removal from the throne. This was easily arranged, courtesy of a manufactured charge of high treason against her for adultery with four men and for incest with her brother, George. The outcome was a foregone conclusion, and George was executed two days before his sister, in May 1536. The Bullen family's star had now crashed. Two years later, both Anne's parents were dead and Hever Castle was taken over by Henry, who gave it to his fourth wife, Anne of Cleves, as part of her divorce settlement.

William Waldorf Astor

Hever Castle's second incursion into the history books occurred at the turn of the twentieth century, when William Waldorf Astor bought it. His family had made a fortune in America and he was now happily spending it in Britain, having declared that his native country was 'no longer a fit place for a gentleman to live'. One of his most ambitious projects was to rescue Hever from its wretched and ruinous condition. In

BELOW: The gardens are one of the delights at Hever Castle. In addition to the many examples of topiary, there is a maze, an Italian garden, a rhododendron walk and a water maze.

doing this, he completely restored the building in the most painstaking fashion and also landscaped the gardens, excavated the lake and provided guest accommodation by building the Tudor village. Although this appears to be a collection of individual Tudor cottages that have been built at different times by different people, they were, in fact, all constructed at the same time and many of the buildings are linked internally. The village contains over one hundred rooms, many of which are now available for corporate events.

William Waldorf Astor so beautifully restored Hever that it is difficult to detect any signs of modern conveniences, such as electric light switches and radiators. The rooms have been furnished to reflect their surroundings, using furniture from a variety of different periods rather than exclusively Tudor to give the castle an eclectic, interesting atmosphere. Some of the rooms, such as the Library, even have the feel of a comfortable family home rather than something more suited to a museum.

Extravagant Entertaining

Although there have been great changes to Hever since the Bullen family lived here in the sixteenth century, there are still some areas of the castle that they would recognize, should they visit it today. For example, the Dining Hall would still be familiar as it was the Great Hall in their day. They would have used the Great Hall for large social gatherings, especially when Henry VIII visited the castle and no expense was spared in entertaining him. Although it was advantageous in many ways to have strong connections with a reigning Tudor monarch, not least because of the social advancement and privilege that it promised, it could also be ruinously expensive whenever the royal party came to stay because most of the court would come too. Everyone had to be fed and housed, and there could never be any shortage of good food and wine. Such lavish entertaining ruined many noble families. The Bullens, of course, were ruined for other reasons, but their legacy lives on at Hever in their moated medieval castle and in the tumultuous role they played in Britain's royal and religious history.

ABOVE: Henry VIII stayed at Hever several times, and the Henry VIII Room is named for him. The ceiling was built in 1462 and the panelling created about one hundred years later.

CARISBROOKE CASTLE

Several royal palaces in Britain began life in private ownership but were later acquired by the reigning sovereign as punishment for a transgression by the owner; Carisbrooke Castle, on the Isle of Wight, is a classic example of this. Its position, just off the south coast of England in the English Channel, has for centuries made the Isle of Wight a prime strategic point for foreign invaders. If they could land here and secure the island, they had the perfect launch for their final bid to invade England. This point was not lost on the Normans, who invaded England in 1066: they knew that if they could do it, so could other invading armies, and they therefore had to defend their newly-won land with a string of fortresses.

Passing into Royal Hands

There had already been a Saxon fort at Carisbrooke, occupying a perfect position on high ground and close to the River Medina. The Norman lord, William Fitzosbern, built a wooden fort on top of the old Saxon defences but, when his son, Roger, took part in a rebellion against William the Conqueror in 1078, he had to forfeit all his lands as a punishment. Although the castle was now in royal hands, it was once again used as a base for insurrection when, in 1082, William's half-brother, Odo, staged another rebellion against him.

In 1100, Henry I gave the castle to the de Redvers family and also made them lords of the Isle of Wight. They began to build the stone castle that stands here today and Carisbrooke stayed in their family until 1293, when the last owner and lord, Isabella, sold it to the Bishop of Durham, who bought it on behalf of Edward I. Isabella enjoyed a high level of comfort at Carisbrooke, even to the extent of having glass in the windows, which was an almost unheard of luxury at the time because of the excessive cost involved.

Increasing Fortifications

The castle was besieged in 1377 by an invading French army, but they were beaten back after their commander was killed by a single arrow fired from one of the arrow slits. Medieval Britain was a turbulent country, so it was important to keep defensive castles such as Carisbrooke in good condition in case they were needed in a hurry. After the national emergency triggered by the threat of the Spanish Armada in 1588, Elizabeth I carried out works between 1597 and 1602 to make sure that Carisbrooke was adequately fortified.

OPPOSITE: *The thirteenth-century St Nicholas's Chapel has become a memorial to all those who died on the island during the First and Second World Wars.*

BELOW: *The Courtyard in the castle contains many buildings, including the Governor's Quarters (left) and the Well House (right).*

ABOVE: The stone Saxon defences at the bottom of the Norman motte, or earth mound, are still clearly visible.

Prisons and Museums

In an ironic twist of fate, the fortifications paid for by Elizabeth I were eventually used against her cousin, Charles I. In November 1647, during the English Civil War, Charles I decided to escape the dangerous atmosphere of London for what he thought was the safety of the Isle of Wight. Much to his astonishment, and what must have been considerable displeasure for a king who truly believed that he was a god in human form, the governor of Carisbrooke Castle took Charles into custody and held him prisoner here until September 1648. Legend has it that Charles tried to escape by crawling through a window, but the spacing between the mullions was too small and he became

stuck. His daughter, Elizabeth, was also held prisoner at the castle and died here on 8 September 1650.

As the centuries progressed, Carisbrooke was allowed to decline into ruin. Nevertheless, the castle gained another royal patron in 1896 when Princess Beatrice, the youngest daughter of Queen Victoria, who went through her very long life with the nickname 'Baby', became governor of Carisbrooke and set about restoring it as best she could. She introduced the first museum at the castle, and in doing so proved that she had inherited her mother's love for the past and her determination to preserve Britain's royal palaces.

ABOVE: The Norman gateway, which is heavily defended to repel possible invaders, leads into the Courtyard of the castle.

HATFIELD PALACE

atfield Palace was built in 1480 for Cardinal Morton, who was the Bishop of Ely and later Archbishop of Canterbury, but in 1533 it fell into the rapacious hands of Henry VIII who wanted it for his daughters, Mary and Elizabeth. Not surprisingly after her difficult childhood, much of which was spent at Hatfield, Elizabeth I had little interest in the palace and preferred Theobalds House nearby, which was owned by her chief minister, William Cecil, who later became Lord Burghley. Her successor, James I of England and VI of Scotland, also preferred Theobalds House as, by this time, a great deal of money had been lavished on it to make it a fit place for visiting royalty. James suggested to Lord Burghley's son, Robert Cecil, that they exchange properties, and this arrangement took place in 1607.

Under an Oak Tree

History was made at Hatfield Palace in 1558. Late in the morning of 17 November, the young Princess Elizabeth was sitting under an oak tree in the grounds, reading a book. She had no idea that she was now Queen of England, following the death of her half-sister, Mary I, earlier that morning. Elizabeth already had vivid experiences of the dramatic twists and turns of fate, having entered the world in 1533 as a royal princess and daughter of Henry VIII and Anne Boleyn. At the age of two she was denounced by her father as a bastard who had no right to the English throne, and her mother was beheaded. Henry later changed his mind and declared her third in line to the throne after her half-brother, Edward, and her half-sister, Mary, but he failed to declare her legitimate. When Mary I succeeded to the throne in 1553 she quickly became suspicious of Elizabeth, and had her imprisoned in the Tower of London for alleged complicity in a rebellion in 1554. Elizabeth was freed without charge three months later, but Mary always believed that she was guilty.

Hatfield House

Having gained ownership of Hatfield Palace, Robert Cecil, who was now Earl of Salisbury, felt he wanted a house that reflected his importance. He ignored the existing royal palace and began to build a completely new house, in an 'H' shape, further up the hill. He hoped that James and his queen, Anne of Denmark, would visit frequently, so he created a house that was fit for royalty. The exterior domes and turrets were decorated with gold leaf, in case people were left in any doubt about the status of the occupant. There were also staterooms for important ceremonial occasions.

One wing of the original Hatfield Palace still stands in the grounds of Hatfield House, having undergone extensive restoration in the twentieth century. The Tudor banqueting hall in the palace is where Elizabeth I held her first Privy Council on 20 November 1558. Appropriately, considering the later history of Hatfield, William Cecil was appointed Secretary of State at that meeting.

Hatfield House enjoyed its apotheosis during the Victorian and Edwardian eras, when the 3rd Marquess (and 9th Earl) of Salisbury was the British Prime Minister. It became one of the most important and popular country houses in Britain and was once more a thriving hub of political and social activity.

OPPOSITE: *Although only a small area of Hatfield House is open to the public, it is well worth visiting for its atmosphere.*

BELOW: *The Elizabethan knot garden in front of the great hall was painstakingly restored in the 1980s.*

London

*From the delights of the Queen's House in Greenwich to the
grandeur of Buckingham Palace, London is rich in royal
residences. There is something here to suit every aesthetic taste,
whether it is for the purity of Romanesque architecture or the
complexities of Victorian Gothic. Some of the buildings,
including St James's Palace, continue to be working palaces in
which the business of state is conducted daily, while others, such
as Eltham Palace, are now tourist destinations. London's oldest
palace, which was originally built as a fortress, is the Tower of
London: one of the most famous buildings in the world.*

*RIGHT: The Palace of Westminster, on the north bank of the River Thames, is one
of the most famous sights in the world. The many Gothic turrets which adorn the
Houses of Parliament point skywards but are dwarfed by the central spire, which
is actually a ventilation shaft. Big Ben rises in the distance and, beyond that,
Westminster Bridge spans the Thames.*

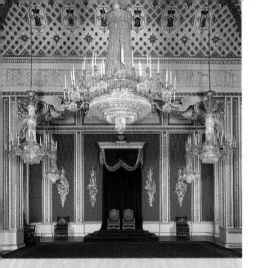

BUCKINGHAM PALACE

Buckingham Palace is one of the most famous royal palaces in the world. Its familiarity has increased since the advent of television as it is the focal point of most major royal events, such as weddings and other ceremonial occasions. Each day, hundreds of tourists gather outside the wrought-iron gates of the palace to watch the Changing of the Guard and each summer the Queen holds a series of parties in the extensive gardens at the rear of the palace. In addition, there are usually twenty investitures each year at Buckingham Palace, in which honours are conferred on celebrities as well as people who are less well known. Such events, however, are merely the tip of a very large iceberg as Buckingham Palace is a working palace, employing 450 people. The business of state is conducted here, with the Queen and the Duke of Edinburgh receiving many guests in both formal and informal settings. The Royal Standard flutters from the flagpole when the Queen is in residence, but it is always business as usual whether she is here or not.

Buckingham House

The first building to stand on the spot that is now occupied by Buckingham Palace was Goring House, erected in 1633 by Lord Goring. It was a country house, on what was then a border of London, surrounded by the greenery of St James's Park and Hyde Park. After a disastrous fire in 1675 it was rebuilt in 1677 as Arlington House, and once again in 1702–5 as Buckingham House, when it was named for its owner, the 1st Duke of Buckingham. When the Duke died in 1721, his widow failed in her attempt to sell the property to the Prince of Wales, who later became George II, but eventually, in 1761, the Duke's son sold Buckingham House to George III for £28,000. George III and his wife, Queen Charlotte, used it as their family home, while the ceremonial life of the court continued to be conducted at St James's Palace. Buckingham House was gradually extended, but by the time the Prince Regent had acquired it, after the death of his mother in 1818, he knew it was not big enough to suit his needs.

The Prince Regent

At the time, the Prince had nearly finished the creation of the Royal Pavilion in Brighton and Carlton House, which lay at the opposite end of the Mall to Buckingham House. He filled Carlton House with the finest examples of French furniture, recently come on to the market after the end of the French Revolution; all of these are in the Royal Collection today. The Prince lavished massive amounts of money on Carlton House but by 1815 he was finding it too small.

Funding the Project

The Prince's acquisition of Buckingham House set alarm bells ringing in Parliament. His previous building projects had run massively over-budget and the country was in straightened circumstances after the enormous expenses of the Napoleonic Wars. In 1819, Parliament gave him £150,000 to develop Buckingham Palace, which fell far short of the £450,000 demanded by the Prince. He was told that Crown property would have to be sold in order to raise additional funds so, in 1825, Carlton House was demolished and the land developed (Carlton House Terrace now stands on the site).

From a Private Home to a Palace

George III died in 1820 and the prince became George IV. In 1821, he commissioned John Nash to start redesigning Buckingham House. The original plan was to enlarge the existing building to create a private house for the king. Work began on this in 1825 by extending the shell of Buckingham House and building a smaller wing at right angles on either side of it. However, as with so many of George IV's ideas, this original plan was no sooner completed than it was eclipsed by his much more elaborate and opulent scheme to create a proper palace. Pity John Nash, who had already fulfilled his brief to build a private home for the king and who was now caught between Parliament, who held the purse strings, and George IV, who believed that he had the right to whatever he wanted. Nash created the desired palace by raising the height of the two wings. In 1827 the empty fourth side of the square contained what we know now as Marble Arch, which was modelled on the Arch of Constantine in Rome and formed the main entrance to the palace. It was moved to its present position at the top of Park Lane in 1851.

George IV died in 1830 and, following a parliamentary inquiry in 1831, Nash was sacked for 'inexcusable irregularity and gross negligence'. Despite the lavish amounts of money that had been spent on the palace, it was not yet finished. George IV's younger brother, William IV, became king and the architect Edward Blore, fresh from designing Lambeth Palace, was commissioned to continue the work but on a far less grand and extravagant scale.

Victoria and Albert

It soon became obvious that Buckingham Palace lacked the number of rooms needed for staff if it was to operate as a fully functioning palace. To remedy this, Blore built new offices in the south wing and added another storey to the main block. When the Houses of Parliament burnt down in October 1834, William IV made the hopeful suggestion that Parliament should move into Buckingham Palace, which he heartily disliked. Much to his disappointment it was decided to rebuild the Houses of Parliament and keep Buckingham Palace as a royal residence. William never actually lived at Buckingham Palace, as it was still partly unfinished when he died in 1837. When his young niece, Victoria, inherited the throne she moved in almost immediately, only to find that many of the windows would not open and there was something very wrong with the drains. By the time Victoria married Prince Albert of Saxe-Coburg and Gotha in 1840 and started a family, the palace still lacked enough rooms to be a family home. The cheapest solution to this was to move Marble Arch to its present position and build an eastern range to the U-shaped palace, thus creating a four-sided palace surrounding a central quadrangle. This work was designed by Edward Blore and carried out by Thomas Cubitt between 1847 and 1850.

Income tax was about to be introduced on a permanent basis and no one wanted to be accused of financing royal extravagance at the expense of its subjects. Selling the Royal Pavilion to Brighton council in 1846 raised some money and, as it was believed that the Pavilion would be demolished, its contents were removed and initially stored at Kensington Palace. Many items were later used to furnish some of the rooms at Buckingham Palace, much to Blore's horror as he considered them to be far too fussy. In the early 1850s, a new southwest block was built to create a massive ballroom with kitchens below.

Life at the palace continued happily for Victoria and Albert, with all but one of their children being born here. Tragedy struck, however, on 14 December 1861 when Prince Albert died of typhoid fever at Windsor Castle. His devastated widow retired into deep mourning at Windsor Castle and Osborne House, and Buckingham Palace was virtually mothballed for decades. It was occasionally used for state occasions and family gatherings, but for the most part it remained ignored. The palace had a brief renaissance during Victoria's Golden Jubilee celebrations in 1887, but once the festivities were over it returned to its shuttered state.

A 'Ritzy' Makeover

Such neglect and disuse meant that Edward VII inherited a very old-fashioned and musty palace when he succeeded to the throne on 22 January 1901. The old century had died, and with it Victoria, so her son wanted to breathe some fresh twentieth-century life into his London palace. He appointed Frank T. Verity as architect and C.H. Besant as designer. Unfortunately, many of their decorative flourishes, which involved a great deal of white paint and elaborate gilding, were completely out of sympathy with Nash's original designs. They can still be seen today in the Grand Staircase, Marble Hall, Ballroom and Grand Entrance. If some of these rooms bear a strong resemblance to early twentieth-century grand hotels, such as the Ritz or Savoy, it is because Edward

PAGE 52: The Throne Room was used as a ballroom by Queen Victoria, who loved dancing. Today it is used for important formal occasions.

PAGE 53: The Grand Staircase was designed by John Nash for George IV and leads up to the state rooms on the first floor of the palace.

VII liked things to look 'Ritzy'. Of course, these Edwardian decorations reflected the taste of their time, just as Nash's designs reflected the taste of the Regency period.

New Façade

Nevertheless, these Edwardian changes cut little ice with Queen Mary, who lived at Buckingham Palace with her husband, George V, between 1910 and 1936. She took a great interest in the contents of all the royal palaces, and worked hard to recapture some of the Regency flavour that had been lost during successive improvements at Buckingham Palace. Shortly after the start of her reign, the Caen stone on the East Front of the palace began to disintegrate because of the polluted London air. The entire front was redesigned and then resurfaced in Portland stone, to make it look more fitting as the principal palace of the royal family. Sir Aston Webb was commissioned to design the new frontage, and he was also responsible for the design of the Queen Victoria Memorial, which was erected in front of the palace in 1911.

The Second World War

Not every royal inhabitant of the palace had treasured memories of it. Edward VIII, who on his abdication in 1936 became the Duke of Windsor, declared in his memoirs: 'The vast building with its stately rooms and endless corridors and passages, seemed pervaded by a curious, musty smell that still assails me. I was never happy there.'

Fortunately, his successor, George VI, had much warmer memories of their shared childhood in the palace. His reign had barely begun when the Second World War broke out, and the palace became an important focal point for national morale. George VI conducted target practice in the garden, much to the alarm of passing courtiers. When it was too dangerous to sleep in London because of the bombing raids, the king and queen would spend each night at Windsor Castle and return to Buckingham Palace early the following morning to give the nation a sense of continuity and solidarity. Their two daughters, the Princesses Elizabeth and Margaret, spent most of the war at Windsor Castle.

One of the most memorable events in the palace's modern history took place on VE Day, 8 May 1945, when the country celebrated Germany's unconditional surrender the previous day. The London streets, illuminated after over five years of enforced blackouts, were thronged with people who converged on the palace and waited cheerfully for the royal family, together with the Prime Minister, Winston Churchill, to appear on the balcony. After the royal family took their final curtain call, George VI asked some young officers to smuggle the Princesses Elizabeth and Margaret out of the palace so that they could mingle anonymously with the crowds and enjoy the atmosphere.

Royal Wedding

Another world-famous event took place at the palace on 29 July 1981, when Prince Charles married Lady Diana Spencer. This royal wedding captured the world's imagination. The Mall was lined with international camera crews, who were quickly

joined by thousands of sightseers, and all eyes were trained on the balcony. As always on such occasions, there are often tantalizing glimpses of the room that lies behind the balcony. This room is known as the Centre Room and has three floor-to-ceiling windows that open on to the balcony, with its commanding view of the Queen Victoria Memorial and the length of the Mall stretching beyond it. The room has strong overtones of the Royal Pavilion, with a central gasolier that would not look out of place there and yellow Chinese wallpaper that was probably originally intended for the Pavilion. George IV died before Buckingham Palace was fit to live in, but how he would have enjoyed standing on the balcony in all his finery, waving to his cheering subjects.

THE TOWER OF LONDON

In its time, the Tower of London has been a fortress, a royal palace, a prison, a place of execution for those of noble birth, a zoo, a mint, an armoury, the repository of the Crown Jewels and a major tourist attraction. William I originally built it, soon after the Battle of Hastings, in order to establish a secure, defensive London base in a country where the Norman Conquest was profoundly unpopular. It was not the only fortress to be built in London by the Normans: they also built castles in the areas we now know as Blackfriars and Ludgate Circus, among others.

Norman Building

When you visit the Tower today and see a large complex of buildings neatly contained within an outer wall, it is natural to assume that it was originally built this way. What you actually see is a mixture of original walls and buildings, and those that were created specifically for the Tower over the centuries. What initially attracted the Normans to the site was the strong city wall that already bordered the River Thames on two sides. The wall was built by the Romans during their occupation of Britain between AD 43 and 410. The Normans, for their part, dug a ditch on the other two sides and then secured it with a timber enclosure to create a roughly rectangular plot, within which they then began to build. The massive White Tower was built by them to be a fortified palace and marked a watershed in architectural history, as it is believed to be the earliest building in Britain to have fireplaces built into the walls. Another innovation was to build latrines into the outer walls. As the White Tower was a royal palace, it needed a chapel and so the Chapel Royal of St John the Evangelist, a beautiful example of Romanesque architecture, was built. It is now the oldest Norman church in the country and although today the walls are plain, it is believed that they were originally painted.

Defensive Structures

The death of William the Conqueror in 1087 left the White Tower unfinished but it was completed during the reign of his son, William Rufus. Successive kings have carried out more work on the White Tower and have also been instrumental in the building of other towers, such as the Wardrobe and Bell Towers. However, it was not until the thirteenth and fourteenth centuries that the Tower of London was given the inner curtain wall, the outer wall and the moat that we know today.

The Tower Becomes Uninhabitable

The last sovereign to use the Tower as a royal palace was James I, who followed a time-honoured tradition by staying at the Tower before his coronation in 1604. By this time it was in a sorry state: some of the roofs had collapsed and had to be repaired in a makeshift fashion. Although James had insisted on being shown around the many buildings, the place was no longer habitable. By the time of the coronation of Charles II in April 1661, the Tower's condition had deteriorated to such an extent that he was unable to stay here. Anxious to keep up with tradition, however, the royal procession rode to the gates of the Tower at dawn on the day of the coronation, in order to at least start the parade from here.

PAGE 58: Traitors' Gate was so-named because prisoners accused of treason entered the Tower through its portals.

PAGE 59: The White Tower is the massive fortress at the heart of the complex of buildings in the Tower of London.

ABOVE: One of the best views of the Tower of London is from the River Thames. The Tower has grown over the centuries, according the whims and needs of successive monarchs.

The Royal Menagerie

For exactly six hundred years, from 1235 to 1835, the Tower was home to the Royal Menagerie. For most of this time, the collection consisted of royal gifts; animals were only bought for the menagerie after 1822. The Menagerie began in 1235 with three leopards, given to Henry III by Frederick II, the Holy Roman Emperor. The choice of creatures acknowledged the three leopards adorning the coat of arms of the House of Plantagenet, to which Henry belonged. Sixteen years later, a polar bear arrived from Norway; the Sheriffs of London had to pay 4d a day for its food. The bear was allowed to fish in the Thames, although it was kept secure with an iron chain. Incredibly, in 1255, Henry's cousin, Louis IX of France, gave him an elephant; an elephant house was built to accommodate the creature and it even had its own keeper. It is believed to be the first elephant ever seen in England. It was buried within the grounds of the Tower.

The collection of animals grew steadily over the years as more creatures were given to the king or queen of the time. The Menagerie was opened to the public during Elizabeth I's reign, and proved very popular until the 1830s when, for a combination of commercial and animal welfare reasons, the royal collection was given to the Zoological Society of London who had recently established a new zoo in Regents Park. This is now London Zoo, one of the biggest zoos in the world.

Involuntary Guests

Other parts of the Tower were also opened to the public during the reign of Elizabeth I, and proved to be an enjoyable day out for most. However, many of the Tower's involuntary visitors had a very different experience of the place. In addition to its many other roles, the Tower was, after all, a prison and fortress housing royal prisoners as well as commoners who had displeased the Crown. The Welsh Prince of Wales, Llywelyn ap Gruffydd, was a captive here from 1241–4. He fell to his death while trying to escape.

During the Wars of the Roses, the deposed Henry VI was imprisoned in the Tower in 1461 and 1470, and again in 1471; during these times the Yorkist Edward IV occupied the throne. Henry died in the Tower on 21 May 1471; it is believed that he was murdered, probably on the orders of Edward IV, while praying in the tiny chapel in the Wakefield Tower. Legend has it that his murderer was Edward's brother, the Duke of Gloucester, who later became Richard III. Another notorious chapter in English history involves Richard and his two nephews, known as the Princes in the Tower.

The Princes in the Tower

After the death of Edward IV in April 1483, the throne passed to his twelve-year-old son, Edward V. Richard was appointed Protector of his young nephew, and placed him and his younger brother in the Tower, for alleged safe-keeping. Richard then had both boys declared illegitimate, on the grounds that their father's marriage was invalid. As a result of this, Parliament invited Richard to take the throne and he was crowned that July; by then, the two princes had not been seen in the Tower for a month. It was widely believed that Richard had murdered them, and he was publicly reviled. Historians have debated the merits of the case ever since. Although popular legend has it that the princes were murdered in the suitably named Bloody Tower, it is more likely that they died in the White Tower. In

BELOW: At the turn of the eighteenth century, many of the records of the Tower were stored, in chaotic fashion, in the Chapel of St John the Evangelist.

1674, the skeletons of two children were discovered during the demolition of a twelfth-century building attached to the White Tower. They were identified as belonging to the two princes and buried in Westminster Abbey in 1678, on the orders of Charles II.

The Bloody Tower

Over the centuries, since being built in the early 1220s, a wealth of legends and grisly tales has accumulated about the Bloody Tower. It originally went under the much happier name of the Garden Tower, but earned its present name during Tudor times because of the widespread belief that it was where the princes in the Tower had died. The upper part of the tower was altered in about 1360, and again in 1603 when it was heightened and an extra floor was added to provide more accommodation for Sir Walter Ralegh and his family. Ralegh was imprisoned here from 1603–16 for plotting against James I, and his family were allowed to live here with him; this was common practice for important prisoners, who lived here in some comfort.

Sometimes, prisoners were confined to the Tower by members of their own families. This was an experience shared by both Anne Boleyn in 1536 and, in 1554, by her daughter, Princess Elizabeth. Anne was sent here on the orders of her husband, Henry VIII, who had grown tired of her and was increasingly desperate to find a wife who could give him a son and therefore ensure the succession. Elizabeth was confined in the Tower on the orders of her half-sister, Mary I, who wrongly believed that Elizabeth had taken part in a rebellion against her marriage to Philip II of Spain. Elizabeth had the good fortune to be released from the Tower but Anne was executed here.

Traitors' Gate

Both mother and daughter entered the Tower through Traitors' Gate, a low gateway in St Thomas's Tower that was originally designed in the 1270s for Edward I to use as a water gate. It became known as Traitors' Gate because prisoners accused of treason entered the Tower through it; for most, it was a one-way trip. Traitors' Gate can still be seen today, and it is easy to imagine the dread with which prisoners passed through it. The timber buildings above it date it from the early 1530s.

Executions at the Tower

Most prisoners of the Tower, who were here under sentence of death, were executed in public on Tower Hill, just outside the Tower's walls, where overexcited and noisy crowds would gather to watch the proceedings. However, seven prisoners were beheaded on Tower Green, within the Tower's precincts, to avoid the chaos that would have ensued if these events had taken place in public. Two of Henry VIII's wives were dispatched here: his second wife, Anne Boleyn, who was beheaded with a sword instead of the customary axe in 1536; and his fifth wife, Catherine Howard, who was executed in 1542. Lady Jane Grey, a hapless pawn of her ambitious father-in-law in a plot to ensure the Protestant succession, was beheaded on Tower Green on 12 February 1554. She had been proclaimed Queen of England on 10 July 1553, following the death of Edward VI four days earlier, and ruled for nine days before Mary I claimed the throne and had Lady Jane imprisoned.

The Chapel Royal of St Peter ad Vincula

The bodies of all seven prisoners, as well as those of many others who died in the Tower, were buried in the Chapel Royal of St Peter ad Vincula, which stands behind Tower Green. The name of the chapel means 'St Peter in chains', and it was built in the twelfth century for the use of Tower prisoners. At that time, it stood apart from the

OPPOSITE, TOP: The first-floor room in the Wakefield Tower is a reconstruction of how it would have looked in the thirteenth century.

ABOVE: The Queen's House, built in 1540 for the king's representative at the Tower, is now the home of the Tower's Resident Governor. It is the only sixteenth-century building to survive within the Tower's precincts.

OPPOSITE, BELOW: This view of the Tower was taken from Tower Hill in the early 1900s.

Tower, and only became incorporated within its walls during the thirteenth century when Henry III had the Tower enlarged. The chapel has been rebuilt twice since then: first during the reign of Edward I, and once again in 1519–20. The chapel was restored in 1876, when it was discovered that the bodies of beheaded prisoners had been buried under the nave and chancel in a fairly random and higgledy-piggledy fashion. They were reinterred beneath the marble pavement that lies in front of the altar.

The Crown Jewels

One of the biggest attractions at the Tower of London is the display of the Crown Jewels. They have been on public display since the seventeenth century. Most of the treasures on show are known as the Coronation Regalia; as their name implies, they are used at coronations. They include the Sovereign's Orb and Sceptre, which were made for the coronation of Charles II after the restoration of the monarchy in 1660. In fact, most of the Coronation Regalia dates from this time as it repaced all the regalia that was melted down after the execution of Charles I.

Not surprisingly, security has not always been as tight as it is today. In 1671 there was an audacious and almost successful attempt by Colonel Thomas Blood to steal the Crown Jewels in the Jewel House. First, he disguised himself as a clergyman and went with his nephew to the Jewel House, where they started chatting to the keeper. They were invited to supper, during which time they admired the keeper's pistols, which he duly sold to them. This was a very clever ruse because it left him unarmed. The following morning, Blood and some friends arrived to view the jewels and easily managed to overpower the keeper. They were busily stealing the jewels when they were disturbed and had to escape. Members of the Tower's garrison caught them all, carrying items of regalia; Colonel Blood had flattened the crown with a mallet and stuffed it in a bag. He insisted upon speaking only to Charles II who was so charmed by him that, rather than punish him, he fully pardoned him and even gave him estates in Ireland and an annual pension.

Tourism

Today, the Tower is still a thriving hub of activity, thanks to the countless tourists who stream through its gates each year. The red-coated Yeomen Warders, affectionately known as Beefeaters, give vivid guided tours in addition to their military duties. Each evening, the Tower reverts to its role as a fortress during the Ceremony of the Keys, in which the outer gates of the Tower are locked and ceremoniously handed over to the Resident Governor of the Tower. It is an impressive reminder that, despite the Tower's role as one of the main tourist attractions in Britain, it is still a fortress that must be protected.

BELOW: The Chapel Royal of St Peter ad Vincula is the oldest Chapel Royal in England. It was defined by Henry VIII as the parish church of the Tower and it still serves this purpose today.

KENSINGTON PALACE

Not far from the roaring traffic of High Street Kensington in London, set amid the dusty greenery of Kensington Gardens, is a seventeenth-century royal palace. In its time, it has been home to several reigning monarchs: William III and Mary II, Queen Anne, George I and George II. It was also the birthplace and home of Princess Victoria, who became Queen in 1837. Kensington Palace is still home to some members of the royal family; in recent years the most notable residents have been Princess Margaret and Princess Diana.

A Private House for William and Mary

William III and Mary II were responsible for the building of Kensington Palace in the 1690s. Both Protestants, they had been invited to take over the British throne in 1688, when the Catholic sympathies of Mary's father, James II, were making him increasingly unpopular. They duly arrived from the Netherlands and James fled to France, apparently running over Westminster Bridge in such a hurry that he accidentally dropped the Great Seal in the Thames.

The new king and queen had not long been established in England before William's delicate health began to suffer at Whitehall Palace, which was then the official London residence of the royal family. Whitehall was very close to the River Thames, which meant that those living there had to endure the appalling stench that arose from it, especially in the summer: raw sewage flowed into it, as it did into every London river.

Renovations had already started on Hampton Court but William and Mary needed a private London home where they could stay each winter to be near the government in Westminster; Parliament did not sit in the summer because of the smell of the Thames. They found the ideal property in Kensington: Nottingham House, a Jacobean mansion that had been built around 1605 and for which they paid £20,000. At the time, Kensington was a small village that 'esteem'd a very good Air'. Work on the house started at once and was overseen by Sir Christopher Wren. A three-storey pavilion was built on to each corner of the original house, and a wing was added for courtiers. William and Mary proved to be impatient new owners as they moved in only a few months after buying Nottingham House, even though building work was still going on around them. A second phase of improvements was carried out between 1690 and 1692. At this point, the building was known as Kensington House, to underline the fact that it was a private home rather than an official palace. Mary did not enjoy her royal retreat for long, however, dying of smallpox at Kensington on 28 December 1694. William instigated the next phase of improvements, in 1695, before also dying at Kensington on 8 March 1702.

The Orangery

William's successor, Queen Anne, also made her mark on Kensington. She was particularly interested in the gardens, and had the Orangery built. Designed by Nicholas Hawksmoor and Sir John Vanbrugh, the Orangery housed tender plants in the winter and was used for court entertainments in the summer, when the plants could be safely left outside. Today, the Orangery is a restaurant for visitors to the palace, and entry is no longer reliant on royal invitation.

More Building Work

Although Queen Anne conceived 19 children and had five live births, none of her children outlived her, so, when she died at the palace on 1 August 1714, the succession passed to her third cousin, Prince George of Hanover. Anne's death marked the end of the House of Stuart and the beginning of the reign of the House of Hanover. George I inherited the British throne through his mother, Sophia, who was a Protestant granddaughter of James I. Sophia had hoped to succeed to the crown herself, but she died a few weeks before Queen Anne and the throne passed to George. In preparation for his eventual succession, he had already become a naturalized British subject in 1705. When

George I arrived in Britain, Kensington Palace became his London home. He instigated a new round of building, and was responsible for the creation of the Cupola Room, the Privy Chamber and the Withdrawing Room. In total, so much work was carried out under George's instructions that he was never able to make full use of Kensington; the place was habitually overrun with builders who were carrying out his orders.

George II and George III

His son, George II, was the last reigning monarch to live at Kensington Palace. He was very conscious of the unpopularity of the new Hanoverian kings and wanted to underline his English nationality. Before addressing Parliament for the first time after he became George II in 1727, he felt compelled to announce, in his heavy German accent: 'I have not a drop of blood in my veins which is not English.' On average, George II spent a good part of each year at Kensington, although large areas of the palace were locked up after the death of his wife, Queen Caroline, in 1737. Much work was carried out on the palace gardens during his reign, including the creation of the Round Pond in Kensington Gardens, on which generations have since sailed their model boats.

After George II died at the palace on 25 October 1760, it fell into disrepair. George III preferred Buckingham Palace and was really only interested in Kensington for the art treasures that it contained, many of which he began to transfer to other royal palaces. Gradually, the place became denuded and neglected, a state in which it remained until the end of the eighteenth century when accommodation was needed for various members of the royal family. Lavish amounts of money were then spent on refurbishing Kensington in order to make it habitable again.

The Wayward Duke

One of the new residents was Edward, Duke of Kent. He was the fourth son of George III and, like his brother the Prince Regent, had a marked ability to run up massive debts, which even resulted in his having to leave the country for Brussels in 1816. Long before this embarrassing event took place, however, he insisted that his new residence should undergo extensive building work; this was carried out by James Wyatt. Among the rooms that were created was the Red Saloon on the ground floor.

When the Duke of Kent moved into Kensington Palace he was a bachelor, but the sudden death of Princess Charlotte, the daughter of the Prince Regent, in 1817 concentrated his mind on marriage. It was essential to produce a future heir to the throne, as there was not a single legitimate child among all 12 of George III's descendants. Something had to be done so, in 1818, the Duke of Kent married Victoria, the German Dowager Princess of Leiningen. Their only child, Princess Victoria, was born at Kensington Palace on 24 May 1819, and the family continued to live here. Sadly, the Duke was only able to enjoy family life for a few months as he died in January 1820, shortly before the death of his father.

Victoria

Princess Victoria grew up in Kensington Palace. Her canny mother managed to increase their living space by requisitioning

many of the State Apartments, including the King's Gallery, which she converted into three smaller rooms. She and her daughter eventually occupied 17 rooms, much to the disapproval of William IV. When he died in the early hours of 20 June 1837, Princess Victoria was woken with the news that she had become queen. She held her first Privy Council in the Red Saloon on the same day. She and her mother moved from Kensington Palace to Buckingham Palace the following month, and she wrote in her journal: 'It is not without feelings of regret that I shall bid adieu forever to this my birthplace, to which I am really attached.' This was very typical of Queen Victoria, who went through life with one eye on the future and the other on the past.

Open to the Public

The sudden departure of Queen Victoria meant that Kensington Palace once again fell into disrepair. It became a massive repository for anything valuable that was not wanted in other palaces, and it also developed dry rot. By the 1890s, the fate of the palace hung in the balance, with suggestions that it should be pulled down, but eventually Parliament paid for its restoration with the proviso that it be opened to the public.

Today, members of the royal family who live at Kensington Palace have private apartments that are well away from the areas that are open to the public. When visiting the palace and viewing the State Apartments, it is tempting to think of the entire building as a museum rather than a thriving network of offices and private homes. Nevertheless, it is a fascinating insight into the workings of another age. For instance, the State Apartments were laid out in such a way that only the most privileged visitors were allowed to penetrate the rooms that were furthest away. There were separate apartments for the king and queen, with the king's apartments being the more lavish of the two.

The King's Grand Staircase

Originally built for William III by Sir Christopher Wren in 1689, the King's Grand Staircase was used by people visiting the king. The simple, plain walls and oak treads were completely altered in George I's reign to what we see today. The *trompe l'oeil* on the walls was painted by William Kent and shows an arcaded gallery crammed with George I's courtiers. The ceiling is painted to look like a dome, with more courtiers gazing down at whoever is walking up the stairs. Some Yeomen of the Guard are also portrayed on the staircase, wearing their summer uniform, which is similar to that worn today by Yeomen of the Guard at the Tower of London. Anyone visiting the king would first have had to pass the forty Yeomen who thronged the Guard Chamber on the ground floor, before climbing the King's Grand Staircase and meeting more Yeomen at the top.

The King's Presence Chamber

After visitors to the palace had been allowed to walk up the King's Grand Staircase, they entered the King's Presence Chamber. This was designed to be as imposing and lavish as possible, in order to impress upon visitors the might and majesty of the king. In the eighteenth century, the central focus of the room was the throne, placed under a decorative damask canopy.

The walls were hung with tapestries, although they are now decorated with seventeenth-century silk embroideries. The most striking feature of this room is the remarkable ceiling, painted by William Kent in 1724 in the 'grotesque' style that was so fashionable at the time. It is square, divided by four red diagonals, with a central roundel showing Apollo, the Sun god, riding in his chariot. The choice of god was no accident, as it implied that George I was the Apollo of his day.

The Inner Sanctum

In the eighteenth century, a royal palace was like a mini city, full of people going about their business. Courtiers attended to the needs of the royal family, a string of visitors called on the king and queen, and members of the royal household were busy behind the scenes making sure that life ran as smoothly as possible. Both the king and queen had a number of staterooms in which they received their guests, who in turn measured their status by how far they were able to penetrate the inner sanctum of the palace. Some only got as far as the King's Presence Chamber but others, who were better dressed, were received in the King's Privy Chamber, while courtiers would meet the king in the King's Drawing Room.

The Cupola Room

The first room to be decorated by William Kent for George I was the Cupola Room, and the work was carried out in 1722. This was the main stateroom, used for the most important occasions, so it was essential that it should look the part. Kent chose the

OPPOSITE: In 1819, the Cupola Room was the scene of the christening of the infant Princess Victoria, daughter of the Duke and Duchess of Kent, who became Queen Victoria in 1837.

ABOVE: Queen Victoria's Bedroom is full of her personal mementoes, including portraits of her children and a bust of Prince Albert.

theme of Ancient Rome, with its implication that George was a latter-day Caesar. In order to stress George's legal right to the British throne, Kent painted the Star of the Order of the Garter in the centre of the ceiling. Today, the room is dominated by the clock, made by Charles Clay and John Pyke, which belonged to Augusta, Princess of Wales, the mother of George III.

The King's Drawing Room and Gallery

The King's Drawing Room was the most important of the state apartments because it was the pivot of court life. This was where most of the king's subjects would see him. In fact, it served as an unofficial demarcation line because only courtiers and advisors could penetrate further into the palace. The ceiling, painted by William Kent in 1723, shows Jupiter, which was yet another flattering comparison to George I.

The King's Gallery was designed as a gallery for paintings from the Royal Collection. It was originally built for William III in 1695 but has recently been restored to show how it looked in George I's reign, when it had red damask walls and curtains, and gilded woodwork. Many of the paintings are still hanging in the positions chosen for them by George I and William Kent. Looking at this imposing, regal room today it is hard to imagine that it was divided into a sitting room, study and ante-room for Princess Victoria when she lived here.

Queen Victoria's Bedroom

Victoria's bedroom is now known as Queen Victoria's Bedroom, although it was originally the King's State Bedroom. On the death of her uncle, William IV, on the morning of 20 June 1837, the young princess was woken and told that she had become queen. Another queen made her first appearance in this room thirty years later, in 1867, when the Duchess of Teck (a granddaughter of George III) gave birth to her daughter, Victoria Mary. She grew up to marry George V, who was the grandson of Queen Victoria, and became Queen Mary. This was her second royal betrothal as she was originally engaged to her future husband's elder brother, the Duke of Clarence, until his death in 1892. She was very regal, and the political diarist, Henry 'Chips' Channon, recorded that being in her company 'was like talking to St Paul's Cathedral'. As Queen Mary she took an active interest in Kensington Palace, and was responsible for the redecoration of Queen Victoria's Bedroom, the Ante Room and the Duchess of Kent's Dressing Room in 1932–3.

Queen Mary's Gallery

Queen Mary's Gallery was named for Mary II. It is not as ornate as the King's Gallery, but it was an important room for her because it was where she was able to enjoy her many hobbies. Mary had been an assiduous collector of porcelain since 1677, when she married William. Items from her extensive collection were arranged in as many places within the palace as possible; she even placed them on shelves over doors. They also adorned her other homes, at Het Loo and Honselaersdyck in the Netherlands, and at Hampton Court, where many are still on show. After Mary's early death in 1694, William shipped Mary's porcelain collection from Kensington Palace to the house of his dear friend, Arnold Joost van Keppel, in The Hague. Sadly, many of these items were later destroyed in a fire.

A Story of Life Through the Centuries

There are many rooms to visit at Kensington Palace, and they tell a fascinating story of life here through the centuries. There is the richness and splendour of the King's State Apartments, which contrast vividly with the simple style of such personal rooms as Queen Mary's Dining Room. Together, they create a memorable picture of life in a royal palace that was partly a private home and partly a building in which state business was carried out.

ST JAMES'S PALACE

The Court of St James, which is the official name for the British court, is administered from St James's Palace in London, even though the official residence of the British sovereign is Buckingham Palace. Whenever a new sovereign accedes to the throne, the proclamation is still made from St James's Palace. This somewhat confusing state of affairs dates from the reign of George III. He bought what was then Buckingham House in the 1760s as his private residence, but it was too small to be a fully functioning palace and so the court continued to operate from St James's Palace.

The Tudors

St James's Palace was built between 1532 and 1540 for Henry VIII on the site of a leper hospital for young women called St James's Hospital. The adjoining marshland was drained and turned into St James's Park. The only surviving part of Henry's original palace is the turreted gatehouse to Colour Court, which stands at the southern end of St James's. His daughter, Queen Mary I, had a particular fondness for the palace and it was here, in 1558, that she signed the treaty that gave Calais back to the French, an event which made her so unhappy that she declared 'when I am dead and opened you will find Calais lying in my heart'. Mary died at St James's Palace on 17 November that same year. Her half-sister, Elizabeth I, did not share Mary's enthusiasm for the palace but she did stay here whenever Whitehall Palace was being cleaned. In July 1588, Elizabeth moved from Richmond Palace to St James's Palace, which was considered to offer greater security, during the time of the Spanish Armada.

Prison, Prostitutes and Turnips

On occasion, St James's Palace was also used as a place of imprisonment. On 29 January 1649, Charles I spent his last night at the palace, and the following morning was led from it, through St James's Park, to his execution at the Banqueting House. The previous year, Charles's younger son, the Duke of York (later James II), was also held captive at the palace but escaped during a game of hide and seek with his siblings.

In 1698, Whitehall Palace was destroyed by fire and St James's Palace became the main royal residence in London. Queen Anne was born here on 6 February 1665 and spent a great deal of time here during her lifetime. St James's Park had increased in size over the years and was now open to the public, although by Anne's reign it was a notorious haunt for prostitutes. Anne died in 1714 and George I succeeded to the throne. He had a tremendous passion for agriculture and is reputed to have asked a minister how much it would cost to close St James's Park to the public and grow turnips there instead. The ironic answer was: 'Only three crowns, Sire.'

The Monarch Moves out of the Palace

In 1814, during the celebrations following the defeat of Napoleon, the Prussian Colonel-in-Chief, Marshal Blücher, stayed at St James's Palace. The public could see in through the windows of his apartment and it is said he enjoyed bowing to those who strolled past. George IV had little interest in the palace, being caught up in more exciting projects, such as the building of Buckingham Palace and the renovations at

Windsor Castle. However, he did commission John Nash to remodel the state apartments between 1820 and 1824. George certainly had no intention of living here himself, setting a precedent that was followed by all succeeding monarchs.

Nevertheless, two of George's brothers lived in houses built on opposite sides of Stable Yard Road within the precincts of the palace: the Duke of York lived at York House (which later became Stafford House and is now known as Lancaster House) and the Duke of Clarence (who became William IV in 1830) was installed at Clarence House, which was built specially for him by John Nash between 1825 and 1827. The architecture of Clarence House was markedly different from that of St James's Palace, which had retained its Tudor appearance despite the work of later architects such as John Vanbrugh and Nicholas Hawksmoor. William IV continued to live at Clarence House throughout his seven-year reign, and a first-floor passage was built to link his home with the state apartments in St James's Palace. The king could not abide Buckingham Palace and had attempted to live in St James's Palace but found it was so small that he and his wife, Queen Adelaide, had to move all their books and letters out of their rooms before they could hold any levées.

The Chapel Royal and Clarence House

Today, St James's Palace is the London home of the Princess Royal, and also of Princess Alexandra and her husband, Sir Angus Ogilvy. It is a working palace, housing several official departments. The palace also contains the Chapel Royal, which was built by Henry VIII and renovated in 1836. The term 'Chapel Royal' originally did not refer to a chapel itself but to the priests and singers who catered for a king or queen's spiritual needs. The Chapel Royal at St James's Palace has therefore seen some very illustrious musicians in its time, including Handel, who was a composer for George II.

Clarence House has provided a home for various members of royalty: Queen Victoria's mother, the Duchess of Kent; Victoria's second son, Alfred, Duke of Edinburgh; and her third son, the Duke of Connaught. It also became the London home of the then Princess Elizabeth and Prince Philip, Duke of Edinburgh, in June 1949. Before they moved in it needed complete renovation, which was complicated by post-war rationing and bomb damage. All the old, fusty Victorian decorations were removed and replaced by a modern, clean, unfussy look. Princess Elizabeth became Elizabeth II on 6 February 1952, following the death of her father, George VI. She and her young family moved to Buckingham Palace and Clarence House was prepared for her mother, who was now the Queen Mother and who moved into Clarence House with her younger daughter, Princess Margaret, in May 1953. Clarence House remained the London home of the Queen Mother until her death on 30 March 2002. After the Queen Mother's death, the Queen decided that Clarence House should become the London home of Prince Charles and his two sons, the Princes William and Harry. It was extensively renovated once more, and its new occupants took up residence in 2003. In the summer of that year, Prince Charles opened some of the rooms to the public for the first time.

PAGE 74: The oldest part of St James's Palace is the Tudor gatehouse that leads to Colour Court, which was built for Henry VIII.

PAGE 75: The Armoury Room has intricately decorated wall panels and a Tudor fireplace, and is adorned with a variety of weapons.

LEFT: Official functions are conducted in the Throne Room at St James's Palace. It is here that the Lord Mayor of London and the Councillors of the City of London present formal addresses to foreign heads of government during their state visits to Britain.

THE PALACE OF WESTMINSTER

The Palace of Westminster has a long and varied history. It was originally the main residence of English monarchs, a purpose it fulfilled for nearly 400 years before catching fire in 1512, forcing Henry VIII to decamp to Whitehall Palace. The medieval palace was almost completely destroyed in another fire in 1834 and the buildings erected in its place are still known collectively as the Palace of Westminster. They are the seat of the British Parliament, housing both the House of Commons and the House of Lords as well as offices for all 659 Members of Parliament.

Edward the Confessor

The first palace to stand on this site, on the banks of the River Thames, was a large, rectangular, fortified building with a moat, built in the eleventh century for Edward the Confessor. At the time, this area was known as Thorney, which meant 'island of briars'. The palace was built on marshland and its proximity to the Thames gave it strategic importance at a period when water was a very efficient means of transportation. Another favourable aspect was that it was far enough away from the rest of London that the reigning monarch could feel safe whenever trouble brewed with his subjects. Edward's palace was also close to the monastery he had built, which today we know as Westminster Abbey. Edward died in the palace at the very beginning of 1066, and in doing so set off a sudden chain of revolutionary events: by the end of that year, England had had three successive kings, and had been invaded by the Normans.

William the Conqueror

Before he died, Edward had named his brother-in-law, Harold, Earl of Wessex, as his successor. Harold was crowned King of England in January 1066 but there were others who also believed they had been promised the English throne, most notably William, Duke of Normandy. William was fully prepared to fight for what he wanted, so he raised an army, sailed to the south coast of England and defeated Harold at the Battle of Hastings in October of that year. In one fell swoop, William ended the dynasty of Saxon kings that had ruled England for so long. He united England with Normandy and introduced many French customs and ideas. Above all, he knew he had to subjugate his new kingdom in order to control it, and this he did with a heavy hand. First, however, William had to make his new position official, so he had himself crowned in Westminster Abbey on Christmas Day, 1066, just over two months after his victory at the Battle of Hastings. His coronation set a precedent, as it was the first to be carried out in Westminster Abbey; since then, virtually every British monarch has been crowned there.

Westminster Hall

William moved into Westminster Palace and, in due course, his son William Rufus took up residence there as William II. He wanted to enlarge and improve it, but he was only able to build Westminster Hall before his untimely death in 1100. This was a period of English history when kings and heirs seemed happy to plot against their rivals, and William is believed to have been shot in the back by a supporter of

PAGE 78: *The Queen's Robing Room is where the Queen puts on her robes before the State Opening of Parliament. It is decorated with frescoes depicting Arthurian legends.*

PAGE 79: *The Gothic buildings that make up the Palace of Westminster were designed by Charles Barry and Augustus Pugin in the mid 1800s, to replace the medieval buildings that were destroyed in a fire in October 1834.*

RIGHT: *The Lord's Chamber belongs to the House of Lords, also known as the Upper House. It is here that the Queen attends the State Opening of Parliament each November.*

BELOW: *Westminster Bridge was the second masonry bridge to span the Thames, and was opened in 1750. In 1862 it was replaced by the cast-iron bridge shown in this Victorian photograph.*

his younger brother Henry, who promptly inherited the crown and became Henry I.

Westminster Hall was built at the northern end of the palace, with the domestic apartments at the eastern and southern ends, and is the only part of the original palace still standing. When Westminster Hall was completed in 1099, William Rufus complained about its size, saying that it was a 'mere bedchamber' in comparison to what he had been expecting. This was some bedchamber: the Hall consisted of a central nave, 73 metres (240 feet) long, almost 12 metres (40 feet) high and with a gallery that ran all around it. The walls were over 1.8 metres (6 feet) thick. At the time, it was the largest hall in Europe. Succeeding kings have also made their mark on it: Edward II had it restored after a fire in 1291, and Richard II increased the height of the walls by 0.6 metres (2 feet). He was also responsible for the oak hammerbeam roof, which is 28 metres (92 feet) high in the centre and was a magnificent feat of medieval architecture. It is still one of the largest unsupported roofs in the world.

Although Westminster Hall was originally used as a banqueting hall, particularly for coronations, between the thirteenth and nineteenth centuries it also contained the Law Courts. Curiously, these were joined in the mid 1600s by stalls selling a variety of goods, including books. On occasion, the traders would conduct their business while momentous events in English history were taking place in the nearby courts. The trials of Sir Thomas More and Anne Boleyn, who both fell foul of Henry VIII, were held here in 1535 and 1536 respectively, and Guy Fawkes also stood trial here in 1606, after his abortive attempt to blow up the House of Commons with the King and Parliament in it. In 1649, in a trial that would forever change the relationship between the English people and their monarch, Charles I was convicted here of treason and sentenced to death.

Westminster Hall is still in use today, as the vestibule of the House of Commons. It featured prominently in 1979 during celebrations to mark the Queen's Silver Jubilee, and also in 1995 during the fiftieth anniversary of the end of the Second World War. It was the site of the lying-in-state of Edward VII in 1910, Sir Winston Churchill in 1965, and Queen Elizabeth the Queen Mother in 2002.

The British Parliamentary System

The medieval palace was not only the home of the reigning sovereign, it was also the site of Parliament and the Law Courts, so the buildings were designed accordingly. The palace has seen the development of the British parliamentary system, which is widely copied throughout the world. In medieval times, the monarch was advised by the Royal Council, which consisted of bishops and nobles. This eventually led to the formation of the House of Lords. The House of Commons was the natural development of a council of lesser personages, such as burgesses and knights, who began to meet independently of the Royal Council. From 1550, the House of Commons met in what had been the Royal Chapel of St Stephen until it was deconsecrated in 1547.

One of the few areas of the Palace of Westminster that has survived over the centuries is Old Palace Yard. It has been the address of some notable people, including Geoffrey Chaucer, when he was Clerk of the King's Works, and Ben Jonson. Old Palace Yard has also been the site of executions, such as those of Guy Fawkes and Sir Walter Ralegh.

Fire at the Palace

Various fires have destroyed much of the original medieval Palace. In 1512, following a fire, Henry VIII moved out of the Palace of Westminster into Whitehall Palace. He was the last sovereign to live at the Palace and the royal apartments were taken over by parliamentary officials. Nevertheless, the building continued to be called a royal palace, and is still regarded as such today. In October 1834, fire once again swept through the medieval palace, and this time it was virtually destroyed; only the crypt of St Stephen's Chapel, the Jewel Tower and Westminster Hall survived. This was disastrous, but it was also an opportunity for some imaginative redevelopment. Charles Barry and Augustus Pugin were the architects, and they created the Gothic buildings that we know today.

OPPOSITE: The Arthurian frescoes in the Queen's Robing Room were painted by William Dyce in 1841, after he successfully competed for the honour.

ABOVE: The Victoria Tower Gardens take their name from the Victoria Tower which overlooks them from the Palace of Westminster. The tower was badly damaged during the German air-raid that demolished the House of Commons on 10 May 1941.

ELTHAM PALACE

There have been two great flowerings in the life of Eltham Palace. The first lasted for three centuries, between the reigns of Edward II and Elizabeth I, when it was one of the great medieval English palaces. The second occurred in the 1930s when the Courtauld family, the people who lived here at the time, turned it into a fine example of Art Deco splendour. Today, Eltham Palace offers an extraordinary contrast of styles, each richly evocative of particular periods in English history.

Medieval Royalty

Eltham, now a busy suburb of London, has the distinction of being mentioned in the Domesday Book as the property of Odo, Bishop of Bayeux (the half-brother of William the Conqueror). At this time a moated manor house stood on the site and was given to Edward II when he was still Prince of Wales in 1305. In due course, the house passed to his wife, Queen Isabella, who spent much of her time here. Known in her own lifetime as the 'She Wolf of France', Isabella was ambitious and scheming. Edward's marriage to her ensured an alliance with the French, as her father was King Philip IV of France, but it also led to his murder at Berkeley Castle, over which Isabella conspired with her lover, Roger Mortimer.

During the reign of Richard II, in the fourteenth century, improvements were made to Eltham under the guidance of Geoffrey Chaucer, who was the clerk of works. In 1402, Henry IV was married by proxy here to Joan of Navarre. Some of the most significant changes to Eltham Palace were carried out by Edward IV, including the building of the Great Hall in the 1470s. This room has the third largest hammerbeam roof in the country, and was the scene of many royal celebrations and feasts.

The last medieval king to enjoy himself at Eltham was Henry VIII, who spent a large part of his boyhood here. As he got older, he spent less and less time here; his daughter, Elizabeth I, also became an infrequent visitor as she preferred to be at Greenwich Palace, which was nearby.

Leaving Royal Hands

Eltham passed out of royal hands altogether during the Interregnum that followed the execution of Charles I in 1649, because it was seized by Parliament. By this time it was described as being 'much out of repair', and was sold to Colonel Nathaniel Rich who began to demolish it. After visiting the palace in 1656, the diarist John Evelyn recorded: 'Both the palace and chapel in miserable ruins, the noble wood and park destroyed by Rich, the Rebel.' The next owner was Sir John Shaw, who left the remains of the palace to moulder and built Eltham Lodge in the grounds instead. He used the Great Hall as a barn, a function that it continued to perform for the following two centuries, even after a campaign to protect it from demolition in 1827.

A Renaissance at Eltham

The renaissance of Eltham Palace began in the 1930s when a wealthy couple, Stephen and Virginia Courtauld, bought it and built a highly contemporary house next to the Great Hall. The house was the last word in Art Deco architecture and formed a stunning contrast to the splendours of the medieval hall that stood beside

it. The Courtaulds paid equal attention to the gardens and laid out a sunken rose garden, a rock garden, a spring bulb meadow and a woodland garden. They left Eltham Palace in 1944, when it was taken over by army educational units that stayed

PAGE 84: In the fifteenth-century a bridge was built to span the moat at Eltham. In the 1930s, the moat was incorporated into the landscaped gardens.

PAGE 85: The Great Hall has miraculously survived an eventful history, including being turned into a barn. Its two original fireplaces can now be found in pubs in Eltham.

RIGHT: The Courtaulds' modernist 1930s house, designed by Seely and Paget, adjoins the medieval Great Hall.

here until 1992. In 1995 English Heritage acquired Eltham Palace and spent four years restoring it before opening it to the public, in all its medieval and Art Deco beauty, in 1999.

THE BANQUETING HOUSE

The Banqueting House in Whitehall, London, is an exquisite gem of royal architecture. Inigo Jones built it between 1619 and 1622, and it was at the forefront of an architectural revolution that gradually transformed London from a medieval jumble of timber and brick houses to a city of stone buildings, inspired by ancient Rome and contemporary Italian design. In 1649, it was the scene of another great revolution when Charles I was executed here; an event that threw Britain into a decade of republicanism. Taking place 140 years before the French embarked upon their own notorious revolution, it shocked the world and was a turning point in the relationship between the British monarchy and its parliament: from the Restoration in 1660 onwards, the balance of power changed forever.

From Palace to Banqueting House

The Banqueting House is all that remains of the medieval Whitehall Palace built by Henry VIII. He had acquired what was then York Place, the official London residence of the Archbishops of York, as a penance from Cardinal Thomas Wolsey in 1529. Henry moved into York Place within ten days of Wolsey giving it to him, renamed it Whitehall and immediately began a massive expansion programme. By the time of Henry's death in 1547, Whitehall was the biggest palace in Europe, stretching for 9 hectares (23 acres). In 1581 a timber and canvas banqueting house was built for Elizabeth I on the site of the present building and this was still standing, in a much-dilapidated state, when James I of England and VI of Scotland took the throne in 1603. Three years later, he replaced the old Elizabethan banqueting house with a building specifically for court masques (theatrical and musical entertainment), but this burned down in 1619. James then commissioned Inigo Jones to build a replacement, which was completed in 1622. Its clean, elegant interior was intended by Jones to resemble a Roman basilica, a design on which many Christian churches are based. James's son, Charles I, who commissioned Sir Peter Paul Rubens to paint nine ceiling panels celebrating the life and reign of James I, embellished this. The paintings also underlined the Stuart belief in the divine right of kings, the very notion that eventually led to Charles's execution.

Execution and Restoration

Ironically, no more masques were held in the Banqueting House after the installation of the paintings in 1636, for fear of them being damaged by lamp-smoke. A new masque house was built at the back of the Banqueting House, which was used principally for diplomatic functions when the galleries and floor would be crammed with onlookers. The street outside the Banqueting House was also crammed with onlookers early in the afternoon of 30 January 1649, when Charles I stepped through a window of the Banqueting House on to a specially built balcony, where he was executed. As the public executioner refused to attend and his assistant could not be found, Charles I was beheaded by two hooded men whose identities have never been

PAGE 88: The Rubens ceiling panels marked the arrival of baroque style in Britain.

PAGE 89: Inigo Jones gave the room classical proportions, making it twice as long as it is wide and high.

ABOVE: The undercroft was designed as a place for James I to drink with his friends.

OPPOSITE: The exterior was refaced in Portland stone between 1829 and 1837.

revealed. It was a bitter winter's day so he wore two shirts, in case any shivers from the cold should be interpreted as those of fear.

When his son, Charles II, was formally restored to the throne on 29 May 1660, his thirtieth birthday, he was received by both Houses of Parliament at the Banqueting House. The crown was once again offered here on 13 February 1689, when the then Prince and Princess of Orange were invited to become William III and Mary II. Whitehall Palace burnt down in 1698 and the Banqueting House was converted into a Chapel Royal. It was used as a museum between 1893 and 1962, but has now been restored to its original, splendid appearance, a small building which has played a major role in British history.

THE QUEEN'S HOUSE

Viewed from the River Thames, the beautiful Queen's House in Greenwich looks like the rather meagre filling in an architectural sandwich, dwarfed as it is between the two, large flanking wings of what is now the National Maritime Museum. There it sits, a perfect Palladian house perched between two much bigger buildings. This is, in fact, something of an optical illusion as the Queen's House actually sits a long way behind the National Maritime Museum, in its own grounds.

Medieval Palaces
There has been a royal palace at Greenwich since Tudor times; Humphrey, Duke of Gloucester, who was the brother of Henry V, built the original palace in 1427. He called it Bella Court and in 1433 it was enhanced by his acquisition of 80 hectares (200 acres) of what is now Greenwich Park. In 1445 he lent the house to his nephew, Henry VI, and his new bride, Margaret of Anjou, for their honeymoon. They liked it so much that when the Duke died in 1447 they moved into it and renamed it Placentia, meaning 'the pleasant place'. Henry VIII and his two daughters, Mary and Elizabeth, were all born here, in what became one of Henry's favourite palaces.

Inigo Jones and Civil War
In 1603, the thrones of England and Scotland were merged, and James VI of Scotland became James I of England. He settled both the park and the palace on his wife, Anne of Denmark, and commissioned Inigo Jones to design a new palace for her. Jones's design was strongly influenced by the architecture of Andrea Palladio in Italy and he began building in 1616. Work stopped two years later when Anne became ill; she died in 1619, and the incomplete building was given to her son, Prince Charles. He became Charles I in 1625 and, four years later, gave Greenwich to his wife, Henrietta Maria. She instructed Jones to continue his work, and the house was completed in 1640. Henrietta Maria was so charmed by the house that she called it 'the house of delight'.

The palace was built in an H-shape and originally straddled the Deptford to Woolwich road, but this was moved in 1699. Leading European painters of the day, including Rubens and Gentileschi of Pisa, were invited to decorate the interior of the Queen's House but it was barely finished when the Civil War broke out, and in 1642 Parliamentary forces confiscated it. During this time, many of its paintings were sold, and it was used for the lying-in-state of Commonwealth generals.

A Home for Orphans and a Museum
The Queen's House became a royal possession again at the Restoration in 1660, and Henrietta Maria moved back in, living here until her death in 1669. On Charles II's orders, builders worked on extending Greenwich

Palace but he ran out of money and the work was left unfinished; it eventually became part of the National Maritime Museum. When William III and Mary II arrived from Holland to take over the throne in 1689 they had little interest in the Queen's House because of its close proximity to the River Thames (it made William's asthma worse), and it became the official home of the Ranger of Greenwich Park.

In 1808 the Queen's House was sold to the Royal Naval Asylum, which was a school for the orphans of sailors. A year later, the colonnades and wings that run either side of the house were added. The building was taken over by the National Maritime Museum in 1934, and today part of it has been restored to its seventeenth-century splendour.

Opposite: *The Tulip Staircase was the earliest cantilevered spiral staircase to be built in Britain.*

Below: *Inigo Jones described the Queen's House as 'solid … masculine and unaffected'.*

South West England and Wales

There has been a protracted history of insurrection and warfare along the border between England and Wales. Medieval English kings were anxious to quell costly Welsh uprisings and did so through a variety of measures, but Edward I made an unequivocal statement when he created his 'iron ring' of castles in North Wales at the end of the thirteenth century. Such castles as Chirk and Harlech, built by unwelcome English invaders, were bitterly resented by the Welsh people whom they were intended to subdue. Today, these magnificent castles are lasting reminders not only of the tensions between England and Wales but also of the skill of those medieval craftsmen.

RIGHT: *After the Duke of Marlborough's magnificent victory against the French at the Battle of Blenheim in 1704, Queen Anne showed the nation's gratitude by giving him the money to build an equally magnificent palace. However, the relationship between soldier and sovereign turned sour and the Duke had to pay for the final stage of building himself.*

CAERNARFON CASTLE

The formidable, turreted outlines of the castle dominate the skyline at Caernarfon, as they have done for the past 700 years. Caernarfon Castle occupies a prime strategic site at the point where the River Seiont flows into the Menai Strait. The town walls extend in an unbroken line around the original town, like two arms stretching out from the castle itself. Despite parts of it never being completed, it is a magnificent example of a medieval fortress. Today, Caernarfon Castle is a magnet for visitors eager for a glimpse of the past, but when it was built, at the very end of the thirteenth century, the castle served a very different purpose: the subjugation and control of the Welsh people.

War and Power in Wales

Wales had originally been an independent country, divided into three main areas with their own rulers: Gwynedd in North Wales, Powys in central Wales and Deheubarth in South Wales. There had been many battles over power between the different rulers, who periodically also had to repel invasion from the Anglo-Saxons, Normans and Vikings. Gradually, however, the rulers of Gwynedd became the most powerful and demonstrated this by calling their sons the Princes of Wales. One of the princes, Llywelyn ap Gruffydd, later known as Llywelyn the Last, was even recognized as the Prince of Wales by Henry III in 1267. However, when Henry's son, Edward I, succeeded to the throne in 1272, all of this changed. Edward was a powerful ruler with a genius for military strategy, and he was determined to keep the Welsh firmly under control. Llywelyn had reason not to trust Edward, and therefore refused to pay him homage. After protracted negotiations between the two had ended in defeat, war seemed inevitable. The first war of independence broke out between Edward I and Llywelyn in 1277, with another skirmish in 1282, during which Llywelyn was killed. Having subdued the Welsh in what had turned out to be two extremely costly wars, it was essential that Edward maintain the fragile status quo by repairing and strengthening the existing castles in Wales and building many more in North Wales, where the greatest threat lay.

Edward I's 'Iron Ring'

Edward I was returning from a crusade in 1273 when he first met Master James of St George, who later became his chief architect. James of St George had already established his credentials as a master mason, having worked on several great European castles for Count Peter II and then Philip of Savoy. One of his triumphs was St Georges d'Esperanche, which he built for Philip and from which he took his surname. Edward agreed with Philip that Master James should be transferred to his own service, and this duly happened in 1278.

The combination of Edward I's money and Master James's architectural genius is one of the greatest marriages in medieval history. Together, they created what became known as Edward I's 'iron ring' of castles in North Wales. Master James of St George was responsible, either directly or in a supervisory capacity, for all the castles that were built or repaired in Wales between 1276 and 1283. He built Aberystwyth, Beaumaris, Builth, Caernarfon, Chirk, Conwy, Denbigh, Flint, Harlech, Hawarden, Holt,

OPPOSITE: *The Queen's Gate is one of the great gateways into the castle but it was never completed. It was less vulnerable than the King's Gate, so its defences were considered to be less important.*

BELOW: *The Upper Ward was the setting for the investiture of Prince Charles as Prince of Wales and Earl of Chester in July 1969. His uncle, the Earl of Snowdon, stage-managed the ceremony.*

RIGHT: *Despite receiving heavy bombardments at various times during their history, the town walls at Caernarfon still form an unbroken line around the castle.*

Rhuddlan and Ruthin; and repaired Castell y Bere, Criccieth, Dolwyddelan and Hope. This extensive building programme, coming so quickly after the Welsh wars, nearly bankrupted Edward, yet he had no choice in the matter. He could afford neither the manpower nor the expense of a third war against the Welsh and, once they had been firmly put in their place, he needed to concentrate on subduing other troublesome regions of his kingdom, such as Scotland.

Work began on Caernarfon Castle in 1283. It was not the first castle to stand on the site as a motte and bailey castle had been built here in 1090 by Robert of Rhuddlan. Its circular mound, known as a motte, became part of the upper ward of the Edwardian castle. To signify its importance as the English administrative centre for the entire region, Caernarfon was made to look very different from the other castles of the time. With its horizontal bands of different coloured stone and its multi-angular towers, it is believed to have been modelled on the fifth-century Roman walls at Constantinople. A bastide town was also created, in common with the other castles of the time, such as Harlech and Conwy. The castle gave protection to the town, which in turn supplied the castle with necessary supplies. Such an arrangement was popular with English settlers, which accorded very well with Edward's plans.

A New Prince of Wales

From the start, Edward kept a close eye on the progress of the building work. He and his first wife, Eleanor of Castile, stayed on the site in July 1283, in large timber-framed apartments that had been built specially for the purpose. They returned the following year, and their second surviving son, Edward of Caernarfon, was born here on 25 April 1284. Their elder surviving son, Alfonso, died that August, making Edward the heir to the throne. On 7 February 1301 he was created and invested as Prince of Wales and Earl of Chester, a move that must have angered many Welsh people who were still chafing under the imposed rule of the English. After all, the hereditary line of their own Princes of Wales had been extinguished with the death of Llywelyn in 1282. The titles of Prince of Wales and the Earl of Chester have gone together ever since.

Welsh Uprising

Meanwhile, work at Caernarfon was progressing, and the town was appointed as the centre of government for Gwynedd, which gave it tremendous strategic and political importance. By 1292, the accounts showed that £12,000 had been spent on the castle and town walls. Everything seemed to be going well until, in March 1294, there was a massive Welsh revolt against their English conquerors, for which Edward I was entirely unprepared. The mass rebellion, involving almost the whole of Wales, was led by Madog ap Llywelyn, who styled himself Prince of Wales. The town walls at Caernarfon were badly damaged in September 1294, and once the mob reached the castle itself they set light to everything they could find. Edward fought back with characteristic martial fervour and by the summer of 1295 he had regained supremacy over the Welsh. Edward I died in 1307 and his son, Edward II, who had been the first English Prince of Wales, became king. Work at Caernarfon continued until 1330.

Saved From Ruin

By the seventeenth century, garrisoned Welsh castles were no longer needed. The relationship between the Welsh and English had improved dramatically under the rule of Tudor monarchs, and in 1536 Henry VIII incorporated Wales into England and gave the Welsh people representation in Parliament. This meant that Caernarfon was in a poor state of repair when it was once again pressed into service on behalf of the king during the English Civil War of 1642–8, and it fell to the Parliamentarians in 1646. Thankfully, a government order to demolish it in 1660 was ignored.

As the centuries progressed, Caernarfon became increasingly neglected. It was finally rescued from this sorry state in the last quarter of the nineteenth century by the deputy-

constable of the time. Further repairs were carried out in readiness for an historic event that took place on 13 July 1911: the investiture of the then Prince Edward (who later became Edward VIII) as Prince of Wales and Earl of Chester.

The Princes of Wales

One of the strongest threads that is woven through the history of Caernarfon Castle concerns the various Princes of Wales, from the original Welsh princes who earned their titles because of the power they exercised, to the English princes of royal blood whose line began with Edward of Caernarfon in 1301. From this point onwards, the title 'Prince of Wales' has always been given to the eldest son of the reigning monarch; where there is no candidate for the title it is withheld by the Crown. The current holder of the title is Prince Charles, who is the twenty-first Prince of Wales. Although not every one of them has been given a formal investiture, the majority of them have been invested in front of Parliament. Two notable exceptions were Edward VIII and Prince Charles, who were both invested as Prince of Wales at Caernarfon Castle, using the Welsh Crown Jewels.

When Edward VIII was Prince of Wales, he was a glamorous, handsome prince who captured the public's imagination and whose character was in marked contrast to that of his stern father, George V. He took his duties as Prince of Wales very seriously, and did his best to reduce what was then a yawning gulf between royalty and the ordinary public. He was often criticized for this, as it was felt that such actions would reduce the mystique and importance of the royal family – on one occasion, he was even taken to task for carrying an umbrella as it was felt that only ordinary mortals did this. On 20 January 1936, upon the death of his father, George V, Edward succeeded to the

throne. He abdicated on 11 December that year, however, in order 'to marry the woman I love' – the twice-divorced Mrs Simpson. It had been clear for a long time that Edward VIII was very unhappy in his enforced role as heir to the throne, and many politicians and courtiers breathed a huge sigh of relief when he abdicated as they had always doubted that he would make a successful king.

The second investiture at Caernarfon Castle took place on 1 July 1969, when the twenty-year-old Prince Charles formally received the title that had been conferred on him in 1958, at the age of nine. By some strange quirk of fate, the investiture occurred on the eighth birthday of his later bride, Diana, Princess of Wales. The Prince had prepared for his investiture, and its significance, by spending a term learning the Welsh language at Aberystwyth University. As a reminder that relations between the English and Welsh had not always been harmonious, this investiture was an opportunity for some Welsh nationalists to show their displeasure in a series of bombings. Nevertheless, the ceremony went ahead and was televised, combining medieval ritual with twentieth-century technology.

OPPOSITE: The King's Gate is the main entrance to the castle. It has twin towers and demonstrates the strength of this medieval fortress.

ABOVE: The Eagle Tower is the most imposing of all the towers. It once contained apartments on three floors.

HARLECH CASTLE

Set high on a rocky crag overlooking Tremadoc Bay in North Wales, Harlech Castle was designed as an impregnable and imposing English fortress, able to withstand the uprisings of the Welsh people over whom it presided. With its thick walls and towering battlements, it conveys its intention of Welsh subjugation very eloquently. The architect was Master James of St George, a Savoyard engineer who superintended the building of all of Edward I's castles in Wales. He was even constable of Harlech from 1290–3, as well as being master of works here.

Welsh Subjugation

Edward I considered that his 'iron ring' of castles was essential if his plan to subdue and conquer North and West Wales was to succeed. Wales had originally been a collection of autonomous kingdoms, but from 1200 it became one political unit under the leadership of Llywelyn ap Iorwerth, also known as Llywelyn the Great, who was the ruler of Gwynedd. Llywelyn was even recognized by King John, who allowed him to marry his illegitimate daughter, Joan, in 1205. In 1267, his grandson, Llywelyn ap Gruffydd,

signed a treaty recognizing Henry III as the overlord of Wales. However, he refused to pay homage to Henry's son, Edward I, when he succeeded to the English throne in 1272, thereby triggering the start of many wars between the Welsh and English. Edward knew that he had to use a firm hand with the Welsh, so he built a ring of castles to push home his uncompromising message as hard as possible.

Strong Defences

When Harlech was built, between 1283 and 1289, the castle stood above a creek that led in from the sea. Today, the sea has retreated considerably, leaving Harlech stranded on its rocky prominence. At the time it was built, however, it occupied a highly strategic position, further strengthened by the two walls that encircled it. The only point likely to be attacked was on the landward side, and a massive Gatehouse containing three portcullises, flanked on either side by guardrooms, protected this.

The defensive position of Harlech has been put to the test several times during its long history. In 1404, it faced a massive Welsh rebellion against the English, led by Owain Glyn Dwr, who had appointed himself Prince of Wales in 1400. The Welsh won, Owain Glyn Dwr and his family moved into Harlech Castle, and it is believed that he was crowned Prince of Wales here. In 1408, Harlech was once more under fire, this time from the English, and its outer curtain wall was severely damaged. The English, led by Prince Harry of Monmouth who later became Henry V, eventually regained the castle in early 1409.

Harlech was also involved in the Wars of the Roses between 1455 and 1485, when it was a stronghold of the Lancastrians. In 1468 it came under siege by the Yorkists, who eventually captured the castle. It is said that the traditional song, 'Men of Harlech', was written about this siege.

Damage and Repair

Such skirmishes caused a great deal of structural damage, and more was inflicted during the Civil War of 1642–8, when Harlech was a Royalist stronghold. It endured a lengthy siege from Parliamentary forces between June 1646 and March 1647, when it finally surrendered. By this time, the castle was in such a state of disrepair that its demolition was ordered, but thankfully never implemented. It remained a picturesque semi-ruin until after the First World War, when the Office of Works carried out considerable repairs. Today, the castle is the responsibility of Cadw, Welsh Historic Monuments, and it is still an impressive sight.

PAGE 102, TOP: Despite the semi-ruined state of the castle, the Gatehouse is still very imposing.

PAGE 102, BOTTOM: The Gatehouse leads into the Inner Ward. The six windows in the Gatehouse were all reduced in height at some point in their history.

PAGE 103: Rising above the land around it, Harlech Castle has a panoramic view of the surrounding countryside.

LEFT: The serene setting of Harlech Castle belies its blood-soaked history.

BLENHEIM PALACE

Although it is called a palace, Blenheim was not built for a sovereign. It was, however, a royal gift as Queen Anne awarded a grant of £240,000 of her own money to John Churchill, the 1st Duke of Marlborough, towards the building costs. Anne had good reason to be grateful to him, as he had led his troops to a resounding victory over the French forces of Louis XIV at the Battle of Blenheim, on the north bank of the Danube in Germany, on 13 August 1704.

Blenheim Palace was designed by Sir John Vanbrugh, fresh from completing his previous architectural masterpiece at Castle Howard in Yorkshire. Blenheim was the grandest possible monument to Marlborough's skill as a soldier, and the exterior of the palace was adorned with many architectural reminders of the British triumph over the French. In fact, the building was covered with decorations that symbolized Britain's supremacy over her long-standing foe and the interior was equally imposing, more of a national monument to a great hero than an intimate home.

'Mrs Morley' and 'Mrs Freeman'

Work on Blenheim began in 1705 but it was beset by problems, many of which stemmed from the very close relationship that Queen Anne had with the Duke's wife, Sarah. Anne and Sarah had known each other since childhood, and Sarah became a lady of the bedchamber when Anne married Prince George of Denmark in 1683. Anne, however, was concerned about the difference in status between them, and suggested that they overcame this by calling one another 'Mrs Morley' and 'Mrs Freeman'. Sarah, who assumed the name 'Mrs Freeman' because of what she called her 'frank, open temper', apparently had the upper hand in the relationship because she treated 'Mrs Morley' in a very bossy and dictatorial manner. There has been much speculation (some of it salacious) about the exact nature of the relationship between the two women, not to mention some of Anne's other close female friendships, but, whatever passed between them, their relationship came to a sticky end in 1711 when Anne's loyalty switched from Sarah to her cousin, Abigail Masham.

Financial Crisis

Falling out of favour with the queen came at a bad time for the Churchills. Marlborough's opponents had been steadily undermining his reputation as a Tory politician while he was fighting abroad and, in December 1711, he was dismissed from all his positions and falsely accused of the misuse of public funds. To add insult to injury, some of the money he had been promised for Blenheim failed to appear so, lacking the £45,000 he needed to pay the builders and craftsmen, work on the palace stopped in 1712. After negotiating with the unpaid workmen two years later, the Duke and Duchess of Marlborough resumed work on the palace with their own money.

Unfortunately, the palace was still not finished when the Duke died in 1722. This was deeply provoking to Sarah, who resented having to pay for a house

OPPOSITE: *The North Corridor proves that there is nothing modest about Blenheim Palace, which was built in a triumphalist style.*

BELOW: *The Great Hall displays Queen Anne's arms on the keystone above the main arch, which encloses a minstrels' gallery.*

that she considered to be overblown and fussy, as she preferred much simpler architecture. In 1716 she had had a massive row with the architect, Vanbrugh, who promptly resigned. The palace was finally completed partly by Nicholas Hawksmoor and partly by James Moore, who had made the mirrors for Blenheim.

Winston Churchill

Another great man associated with Blenheim Palace is Sir Winston Churchill, who was born here on 30 November 1874. He was heir presumptive to Blenheim in the 1890s but the title passed to his cousin, the 9th Duke of Marlborough. Like his ancestor, the 1st Duke, Churchill was also responsible for saving the British nation at a time of crisis; when he was Prime Minister during the Second World War. In a newspaper article written in 1966, after Churchill's death, the 10th Duke of Marlborough said: 'Much as Winston cared for Blenheim, it would not have appealed to him to go down in history as its owner – he had other and better ideas.'

LEFT: The Green Drawing Room still has its original eighteenth-century ceilings, which were designed by Nicholas Hawksmoor.

BELOW: A 1905 portrait of Charles Spencer-Churchill, 9th Duke of Marlborough with his wife, Consuelo, Duchess of Marlborough and their sons John, Marquis of Blandford and Lord Ivor Spencer-Churchill, painted by John Sargent.

CHIRK CASTLE

In the thirteenth century, Wales was a dangerous place for the English. Resentment against their English conquerors ran high, leading to periodic outbursts of warfare and insurgence. Any Englishman who wanted to settle in this troubled land had to make sure that his home was strong enough to withstand any attacks that it might receive. One such Englishman was Roger Mortimer, who belonged to the powerful Marcher family. He was given the area around Chirk by Edward I in 1282, after the Welsh were defeated in their second war of independence against the English.

Hostile Lands

Mortimer received further royal assistance when it came to planning the design and construction of Chirk Castle as Edward I's chief architect, the renowned Master James of St George, supervised the building work. The castle was completed and became the home of Roger Mortimer in 1310. Nevertheless, it was added to and improved upon in the following centuries. In the early 1400s, for instance, the south curtain wall was built by Thomas, Earl of Arundel, in an attempt to withstand the army of Owain Glyn Dwr. Glyn Dwr was a guerrilla leader who called himself Prince of Wales and was determined to wrest control of Wales from Henry IV. He led a revolt against the English, which began in 1400 and lasted for twelve years.

Dudley and Myddelton

The castle became a royal possession in 1495, after the execution of the then owner, Sir William Stanley, and underwent various renovations and improvements during the following years. In 1563, Elizabeth I gave Chirk to her adored Lord Robert Dudley. He died in 1588, and in 1595 Chirk was sold for about £5000 to Sir Thomas Myddelton, a founder of the East India Company. The castle has been occupied by the Myddelton family ever since. Sir Thomas's son, who was also called Sir Thomas, became the MP for Denbighshire, which put him on the side of the Parliamentarians during the Civil War. In 1643, Royalist supporters seized Chirk and held it for three years. A few well-placed bribes ensured that the castle was restored to the Myddelton family, this time under the guardianship of the third Sir Thomas. However, he switched his allegiance to the Royalist cause and, in 1659, the castle was once again under attack. This time, the damage was so severe that the upper storeys of the towers had to be completely removed, which accounts for Chirk's slightly squat appearance. Other renovations and extensions were made at the same time, and continued for many years. Today, the grounds at Chirk are extensive and include an area of eighteenth-century parkland.

OPPOSITE, TOP: Chirk is home to many beautiful tapestries and pieces of furniture.

OPPOSITE, BOTTOM: The Great Gallery is one of the most imposing rooms at Chirk.

ABOVE: The grounds at Chirk are extensive, and include a formal garden, a lime avenue and an area of eighteenth-century parkland.

BERKELEY CASTLE

Almost nine hundred years of history have soaked into the walls at Berkeley Castle. It is perhaps not as well known as some other castles, yet so much has happened to it over the centuries that it deserves to be celebrated and recognized as one of the true treasures of Britain. Berkeley was built in the twelfth century, on the orders of Henry II who needed a strategically placed castle that could not only guard the Severn Valley but also act as a defence against the Welsh. In 1153, he granted a charter to Robert Fitzharding to build the shell-keep and the rest of the castle was gradually built around it.

A Place in History

Berkeley Castle is the oldest inhabited castle in England and has been the seat of the Berkeley family since it was built. This old family has witnessed a variety of historical episodes, from major turning points to light-hearted incidents. In 1215, many of the local barons met in the Great Hall at Berkeley Castle before they all travelled to Runnymede in Surrey to sign Magna Carta. In the 1380s, the chaplain here, John Trevisa, believed that the Bible should be translated from Latin into everyday language, so that everyone could understand it. He carried out some of this work in the Morning Room, translating the Bible into the Norman French that was spoken by the Berkeley family at the time. It is also claimed that Shakespeare was so inspired by the castle that he wrote *A Midsummer Night's Dream* in 1595–6 especially for the Berkeley family.

The Murder of Edward II

One of the most notorious events in British history, the imprisonment and subsequent murder of Edward II in 1327, also took place at Berkeley Castle. Edward's wife, Isabella of France, plotted against him with her lover, Roger Mortimer. It is likely that Edward was homosexual but, being heir to the throne, he was forced to marry Isabella of France to ensure the succession. Edward's infatuation with two men, Piers Gaveston and later Hugh Despenser, and the manner in which he favoured them over the powerful nobles of the time, led to a highly volatile situation. Isabella colluded with her lover, Mortimer, who was one of the disaffected nobles, in raising an army against Edward and having him deposed in January 1327. Edward was sent to Berkeley Castle, while Isabella and Mortimer took over the Regency on behalf of her son, who later became Edward III. Edward was imprisoned in the King's Gallery, which at the time was a much smaller room than it is today. In the corner of the room there is a deep hole, with the dungeon directly below it, into which the putrefying carcasses of cattle were regularly thrown, in the hope that their toxic stench would eventually poison Edward; a popular method of murder at the time. The plan failed, however, and he was brutally murdered on 21 September 1327.

ABOVE: This is the main entrance to the castle from the Inner Courtyard. The original Norman doorway is clearly visible above its fourteenth-century replacement.

RIGHT: The gardens are terraced, and the view of the castle from the south terrace shows how it has been improved and embellished over the centuries.

The Midlands and Scotland

For centuries, England and Scotland were fierce adversaries, and this deeply rooted animosity is reflected in the architecture of their castles and palaces. Their royal buildings had to repel attack from enemies and foul weather alike, so they were heavily fortified with very thick walls. Many of these places have a brooding quality that is matched by the events that took place within their walls. Two names crop up again and again, their glamour unfaded by time: Mary, Queen of Scots, who seemed hell-bent on self-destruction; and Bonny Prince Charlie, who vainly persisted in his father's lost Jacobite cause.

RIGHT: *The sprawling mass of Edinburgh Castle towers above Princes Street Gardens and keeps watch over the city below. Each August the Castle Esplanade plays host to the Edinburgh Military Tattoo, which ends with a lone piper on the battlements. It is an important event in the calendar of the annual Edinburgh International Festival.*

LINLITHGOW PALACE

Despite its ruined condition, Linlithgow Palace is one of the most atmospheric and photogenic royal residences in Britain. It sits serenely on a promontory in Linlithgow Loch, with the tower of St Michael's Church rising next to it. The history of the palace is equally evocative, running through several centuries until it was severely damaged by English troops in 1746 after they had succeeded in subduing the supporters of the Jacobite pretender, Bonny Prince Charlie.

Sporadic Building Works

A royal manor house originally stood on the site now occupied by the palace; it burnt down in 1424 in a fire that also destroyed most of the town. James I of Scotland, who had only just been released from prolonged captivity in England, began to build the palace in 1425. The building work went so well that by 1428 he was even able to spend a few days here. Money was no object and the rooms were decorated in the latest fashions. Work was temporarily suspended after James's assassination in 1437, and his successor, James II, had little involvement in the project before his own untimely death in 1460. Nevertheless, the palace must have been in a habitable state at this time because the young James III used it as a residence and gave it to his wife, Margaret of Denmark, as a wedding present in 1469.

The lives of these Stewart monarchs were marked by tragedy, and it struck yet again when James III was assassinated in 1488. His fifteen-year-old son, James IV, inherited Linlithgow and immediately began developing it into a comfortable, modern palace. One of his greatest contributions was to create the west range, containing new royal apartments, which transformed Linlithgow into a four-sided building with a central quadrangle. The palace was also fortified, although on a rudimentary scale, with a barbican built on to the east wall. When James died at the Battle of Flodden Field on 9 September 1513, work at the palace was virtually complete.

James V was born at the palace in April 1512 and succeeded to the throne as a baby. His birthplace was neglected for several years until more work began on it in 1534. Like his father, James V remodelled various areas of the palace, and he moved the main entrance from the east side to the south. He also built an outer gateway, which is still decorated with insignia from the four orders of chivalry to which he belonged: the English Garter, the Scottish Thistle, the Burgundian Golden Fleece and the French St Michael.

Neglect, Fortification and Destruction

Princess Mary, later Mary Queen of Scots, was born at Linlithgow Palace on 8 December 1542, and her father, James V, died at Falkland Palace six days later. At the age of seven months, Mary was moved to the safety of Stirling Castle, and did not set foot in Linlithgow for another twenty years. When her son, James VI of Scotland, also became James I of England in 1603, it was the beginning of a long period of neglect for many Scottish palaces and castles because the court moved to England. Sure enough, the north range of Linlithgow fell down in 1607, and work on replacing it did not begin until 1618. The palace was again repaired in 1633 for a visit from Charles I, and it was fortified by Oliver Cromwell's troops when he stayed here during the winter of 1650. After English soldiers destroyed the palace in 1746, whether by accident or design, it was left in its ruined state. Plans to turn it into a museum or law courts were mooted in the 1890s but these came to nothing, and today Linlithgow is left as a fine reminder of the turbulent Stewart reign in Scotland.

PAGE 116, TOP: The Great Hall contains many interesting architectural features.

PAGE 116, BOTTOM: The north range was rebuilt after it fell down in the early 1600s. It has a Renaissance façade.

PAGE 117: The west range was completed by James IV and contained the royal apartments for James and his wife, Margaret Tudor.

LEFT: Although it is now roofless, the Great Hall in the east range is one of the finest medieval halls in existence.

119

BALMORAL CASTLE

Scotland, declared Prince Albert, was 'very German-looking'. Its wooded hills and valleys reminded him of his native Bavaria and the thought of establishing a private residence there greatly appealed to him and his wife, Queen Victoria. The royal couple had fallen in love with the Scottish Highlands during their visits in the 1840s, not long after they were married, and, although it was a long way from London, the journey had been made much easier by the recent advent of the railway. They were particularly interested in the area around the River Dee, known today as Royal Deeside, partly because it had the lowest rainfall in Scotland.

Life at Balmoral

The acquisition of the estate at Balmoral was not an easy one, with negotiations lasting several years before the sale was finally completed in 1852. There was already a fifteenth-century castle on the site, but it was deemed too small and work began almost immediately on a much grander replacement. White granite, from the nearby quarries at Glen Gelder, was used and the present building was erected under the precise and painstaking direction of Prince Albert, who even went so far as to design a Balmoral tartan. Queen Victoria loved Balmoral, declaring that 'all seemed to breathe freedom and peace'. Both these attributes were very important to her, as she was acutely aware of the need for a private home in which she and her beloved Prince Albert could enjoy a simple life with their growing family, far away from the formality of Buckingham Palace. Both Victoria and Albert were anxious to set an example of Christian family life to the nation, showing that they were willing to work hard for the privileges of their position.

Grief and Friendship

Prince Albert died in 1861 and left Balmoral to Victoria. Soon after his death, his inconsolable widow began to fill the grounds with a series of memorials. There were cairns (pyramids of stones) to commemorate Albert's death and other, happier events, plus statues and seats, but not all the memorials were for Albert. One statue was erected in the memory of John Brown, Queen Victoria's faithful Scottish gillie and a cause of much gossip in her later years.

Four years after the death of her precious Albert, Victoria appointed Brown as her 'permanent personal attendant', and moved him south from Balmoral to Windsor, London and Osborne. At the time it caused great scandal and there were even rumours that the couple had married, with arch references in high society to Queen Victoria as 'Mrs Brown'. Whatever the precise nature of their relationship, there is no denying the easy familiarity that they enjoyed. John Brown often addressed her as 'wumman', and would even tick her off if he thought it necessary. He was also quite prepared to defend her in rows with her family. His alcoholism, combined with Victoria's favouritism, made him extremely unpopular with the rest of the court, although he seemed not to care about such things. Despite his gruff manner, Victoria doted on him.

John Brown died at Windsor on 27 March 1883, from complications caused by his chronic alcoholism, and his death plunged Victoria into deep mourning once again. Her 'true friend' was still not forgotten when she died in 1901. Among the many cherished mementoes that were laid in her coffin were a photograph of Brown and a lock of his hair. Following Victoria's instructions, both of these were placed in her left hand and discreetly hidden by flowers from Queen Alexandra.

A Private Retreat and a Working Estate

Successive generations of royalty have continued to improve the castle and grounds. After becoming king, one of Edward VII's first actions was to have the statue of John Brown moved to a far-off corner of the estate, well out of view. His daughter-in-law, Queen Mary, oversaw the creation of a flower garden and, much more recently, the Duke of Edinburgh created a water garden and enlarged the flower and vegetable gardens. Balmoral is still used by the royal family for private holidays each August and September. Although heads of state occasionally visit the Queen here, Balmoral is principally a private home in which the royal family can relax away from the glare of the camera lens, and indulge their various passions for fishing, painting, gardening, shooting and walking.

OPPOSITE: Prince Albert landscaped the grounds, drawing heavily on his memories of Bavaria. Much of the planting consisted of firs and white poplars from Coburg.

BELOW: Balmoral Castle is part of the Balmoral Estate. This covers about 20,000 hectares (50,000 acres) and is privately owned and funded by the Queen. It is a working estate with strong links with the local community.

FALKLAND PALACE

Built in sixteenth-century French Renaissance style, Falkland Palace was a favourite haunt of Scottish monarchs. It was wonderfully situated for hunting, and a tranquil retreat from the bustle and smells of Edinburgh. The Scottish nobility already knew about the pleasures that Falkland had to offer, as this was not the first palace to be built on the site. Indeed, the foundations of earlier buildings, including a twelfth-century castle, can still be seen to the north of the palace. Life in these older buildings was certainly eventful: David, the son of Robert III, died imprisoned in the castle in March 1402, under suspicious circumstances. He was allegedly starved to death but it is thought he may have died from dysentery.

The land around Falkland was acquired by force when James I of Scotland seized the castle from its owners in 1425, but he appeared to have little interest in it. His son, James II, gave the earldom of Fife to his queen, Mary of Gueldres, and Falkland Palace became a favourite residence of the Scottish court. Mary made various improvements to the palace after the death of James II in 1460, including the creation of what may have been the first gallery to be built in Scotland.

Building a New Palace

In 1501, work started on a new palace, initially under the direction of James IV of Scotland until he died in 1513. The half-finished palace languished, neglected, for several years and it was really only after James V married Mary of Guise in 1538 that any

serious work was carried out at the palace. The work, involving four royal master masons, was carried out very rapidly and much of the existing building was remodelled and new rooms added. Each mason had a slightly different architectural style, which has created some rather interesting contrasts between various parts of the palace. The turreted gatehouse, for instance, has a very different appearance to the medallions and other carvings on the north front of the courtyard.

Unlucky Connections

Work on the palace was completed by 1541, and in April of that year Mary of Guise gave birth, in the palace, to her second son, styled the Duke of Albany. The child died eight days later and the month proved to be a terrible one for Mary and James V, as their elder son, James, also died that April. The king was left without a direct heir, which was a cause of grave concern because it threatened the chance of a peaceful succession; always a matter of prime importance. However, on 8 December 1542 at Linlithgow Palace Mary gave birth to a daughter, also called Mary, who grew up to become Mary, Queen of Scots. Once again tragedy accompanied the birth: James V died six days later at Falkland Palace. Despite these miserable connections with Falkland Palace, both Mary of Guise and her daughter had many happy times here and considered it to be a place of refuge and relaxation. It is said that Mary, Queen of Scots loved hunting to such an extent that deer were moved from one palace to the next, so that there would always be plenty of royal sport. Another royal sport that was enjoyed at Falkland was real tennis, originally called 'royal tennis'. The oldest royal tennis court still in use can be found here, having been created in 1539 for James V.

Although the east range of the palace was destroyed by Cromwell's troops in 1654 and never fully repaired, other parts of the palace still stand and have been restored. The Chapel Royal, the King's Bedchamber and the Queen's Room can still be visited, as can the Keeper's Apartments in the gatehouse.

OPPOSITE, TOP. The painted ceiling of the Chapel Royal dates from 1633.

OPPOSITE, BOTTOM: The carefully-restored Queen's Room in the east range.

ABOVE: The Keeper's Apartments in the gatehouse are open to visitors.

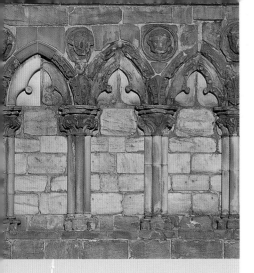

THE PALACE OF HOLYROODHOUSE

The two royal palaces in Edinburgh lie a mile apart from each other, linked by the Royal Mile that snakes its way through the most ancient part of the city. Edinburgh Castle keeps watch from its perch on a craggy outcrop called Castle Rock, while the Palace of Holyroodhouse sits prettily beneath the looming bulk of Salisbury Crags and Arthur's Seat. The two palaces could not be more different in appearance or atmosphere, and it is little wonder that Scottish monarchs throughout the centuries have preferred to live in the picturesque environs of Holyroodhouse rather than in the draughty setting of the castle.

Monastic Beginnings

What we know now as Holyroodhouse began life as an Augustinian monastery, the Abbey of Holyrood, founded by King David I in 1128. Holyrood means 'holy cross', and the Abbey's most important relic was a piece of the True Cross that David's mother, who was canonized in the thirteenth century as St Margaret, had brought to Scotland. Legend has it that, while out hunting, David had a vision of a stag with a cross between its antlers, so he founded his monastery on that very spot.

Such an important abbey needed a guesthouse, and this eventually developed into the palace that we know today. Nothing remains of the early buildings, including the gatehouse that was built by James IV in preparation for his dynastically important marriage to Margaret Tudor, daughter of Henry VII, in the abbey on 8 August 1503. Both kings were anxious to create a greater sense of harmony between their two countries, because the many wars that had been waged between them were expensive, time-consuming and troublesome. In the event, their efforts were in vain as James IV died in battle against the troops of his brother-in-law, Henry VIII, at Flodden Field on 9 September 1513. His wounds prevented proper identification of his dead body, and this sparked off rumours that he had survived the battle, which he had not.

James V

A family pattern repeated itself with each Stewart monarch from James I to James VI; each of them succeeded to the throne at a very early age, sometimes when only a few days old. When James IV died on 9 September 1513, his seventeen-month-old son was crowned James V. James was to have a very important impact on the history of Holyroodhouse, not only because of the building work he carried out but also because the story of his daughter, Mary, Queen of Scots, is tightly interwoven with that of Holyroodhouse.

Between 1528 and 1532, James V built an enormous tower to house the royal apartments. More building work followed between 1535 and 1536, with a new and highly decorative west front. In constructing this,

James was following his father's example of making the palace more habitable for his future bride, Madeleine Valois. She was the daughter of Francis I of France and, despite being in poor health, she represented another important dynastic link between Scotland and other countries. Whereas there had always been an uneasiness between Scotland and England, there was a much greater understanding between Scotland and France: this was, after all, known as the 'Auld Alliance', after the anti-English alliance made between the two countries in 1295.

Sadly, the sickly Madeleine had barely arrived at Holyroodhouse before she died in July 1537 and was buried in the abbey. Anxious to maintain his friendly links with France, James quickly contracted another French marriage, this time to Mary of Guise, the widow of Louis II, the Duc de Longueville. They married in 1538 and Mary was crowned Queen Consort in the abbey in February 1540. Although they had three children, only their daughter, Mary, survived infancy.

OPPOSITE: The walls of the palace and abbey are rich in architectural details.

BELOW: James V's sixteenth-century tower stands on the left of the west front of the palace. It is matched on the right by the tower built over a century later, in 1671.

Mary, Queen of Scots

Mary was only six days old when she became queen, on 14 December 1542, and just under nine months old when she was crowned on 9 September 1543. In the sixteenth century, the children of monarchs were generally treated as pawns in a game of power, dynastic alliance and strategy; Mary was no exception. Half-French through her mother, Mary of Guise, she was married to the young French Dauphin in April 1558 in Paris, and became Queen Consort after the death of her father-in-law, Henry II, in September 1559. Her husband, Francis II, died in December of the following year, and Mary returned to Scotland. However, the religious landscape of the country had altered dramatically, having switched from Roman Catholicism, which she practised, to a staunch Protestantism under the zealous, provocative and extremist leadership of John Knox.

Romantic Folly and Dangerous Plots

After the death of her first husband, it was important that Mary should remarry and, being so eligible, she held the ultimate trump card. This was a source of great worry to her cousin, Elizabeth I, who feared that Mary would marry into one of the great

European Roman Catholic royal families, thereby creating a powerful alliance against her. She need not have worried; instead, Mary became completely enchanted by Henry Stuart, Lord Darnley: he was tall and handsome, and she could not resist him. As he was her step-cousin – they shared the same grandmother, Margaret Tudor – they had to apply for a papal dispensation in order to marry. Mary's advisers were against the marriage, but this only fuelled her desire to go through with it. In fact, they were in such a hurry to get married that their wedding took place on 29 July 1565 in the chapel of Holyroodhouse, before the dispensation arrived.

When Mary, who was still only twenty-three, married Darnley she hoped that he would protect, support and guide her. She soon realized, however, that there was little chance of this as he was self-serving, jealous and vain. Shortly before their marriage, Mary had bestowed on Darnley the title 'King of this our Kingdom', and he was called King Henry by the Scots people. This was not enough to satisfy Darnley's ambitions, however; he wanted the crown matrimonial that would give him equal powers to those of Mary and the right of succession if Mary died before she had any children. He also wanted the glory and power without having to fulfil any of the duties: he was often to be found out hunting and hawking while Mary attended to affairs of state. Relations soon became strained between Darnley and Mary, who was now pregnant. She increasingly sought the company of her secretary, David Rizzio, leading to the inevitable gossip that they were lovers.

In addition to her marital troubles, Mary was also having difficulties with some of the Protestant lords of Scotland who were rebelling against her. Matters came to a head in March 1566, when the Protestant lords formed a conspiracy with other interested parties, including Darnley, that would ensure their return from exile, the upholding of the Protestant religion and the crown matrimonial for Darnley. Rumours that something terrible was about to happen reached the ears of Mary and Rizzio, who chose to ignore them. By now, Rizzio was drunk with the power that he held as the queen's favourite.

Murder and Fear

On the night of Saturday 9 March, Mary held an informal and intimate supper party in her apartments on the second floor of the palace. Darnley's apartments were on the floor below, and were linked to Mary's by a narrow staircase. This privy staircase is now hidden behind the Charles II panelling, and is not the current staircase. Darnley and his fellow conspirators bust into Mary's supper room and dragged Rizzio across Mary's bedchamber and into the doorway of the adjoining outer chamber. Here he was frenziedly stabbed between fifty and sixty times and left to die.

Mary realized that her own life was in danger, and moved to Edinburgh Castle in preparation for the birth of her son, who later became James VI, in June 1566. Her marriage was over and she was emotionally involved with James, 4th Earl of Bothwell, who was the sheriff of Edinburgh, but she still needed to deal with Darnley. There were alarming rumours that he planned to seize the baby prince, who at that time was at Stirling Castle, so mother and baby were reunited at Holyroodhouse in January 1567. Darnley, who had been ill in Glasgow, was brought back to Edinburgh: Mary wanted him where she could keep an eye on him so Darnley was installed in an old house called Kirk o'Field, a short distance from Holyroodhouse.

In the early hours of 10 February 1567, an explosion split the air: Kirk o'Field lay in ruins, having been blown up with gunpowder, probably by Bothwell. Darnley's body was found in the garden and was taken to Holyroodhouse, where it laid in state for several days before being buried in the Chapel Royal; he was, after all, a king of Scotland.

Mary's Final Years

Without realizing it, Mary was playing out the final scenes of her life in Scotland. She appeared to be ricocheting from one unwise decision to the next, and she now agreed, under duress, to marry Bothwell. The wedding took place in the Great Hall at

OPPOSITE: The grisaille frieze that runs around the Queen's Bedchamber is thought to have been created for the visit of James VI of Scotland and I of England in 1617. Mary's supper chamber can be seen through the left-hand doorway.

Holyroodhouse on 15 May 1567, only three months after Darnley's death. Both the Pope and Protestant Scotland were outraged, and Mary was forced to abdicate in favour of her son on 24 July. She and her followers crossed into England, where she was captured and held a prisoner by her cousin, Elizabeth I, for eighteen years before her execution for treason on 8 February 1587.

Decline and Rebuilding

Following true Stewart tradition, Mary's baby son became James VI at the age of thirteen months. He succeeded to the English throne as James I following the death of his cousin, Elizabeth I, on 24 March 1603, thus uniting the warring countries of England and Scotland with a single crown. James was now expected to rule his kingdom from England, and so Holyroodhouse inevitably fell into decline.

The state of the palace became even more parlous during the Civil War, when Cromwell's English troops badly damaged much of it. When Charles II was restored to the throne in 1660, he was determined that Holyroodhouse should be repaired. Work started in 1671, directed by James Maitland, 1st Duke of Lauderdale, who was Secretary of State for Scotland. The results were a masterpiece of baroque architecture, combining an elegance and sophistication that were unknown in Scotland at that time. James V's tower was duplicated at the other end of the west front, and new royal apartments were built around a beautiful quadrangle, whose cloisters referred back to the original Augustinian monastery. The old west front was rebuilt and the windows of James V's tower were stripped of their ancient iron grilles and given the latest sash windows.

The interior of the palace was no less stunning, with magnificent plastered ceilings and many decorative paintings. The final grand flourish was delivered by the Dutch painter, Jacob de Wet the Younger, who was commissioned by Charles II to paint a sequence of portraits of the kings of Scotland for the Great Gallery.

Catholic Conversion

Charles's brother James, Duke of York, moved into Holyroodhouse in 1679. He had strong Catholic sympathies, which ran counter to the mood of the times and eventually cost him the throne when he became James II of England and VII of Scotland. He ordered the abbey church to be equipped for Catholic services, but the work was still in progress when he was forced to abdicate in December 1688. William of Orange, James's Dutch Protestant son-in-law, was invited to take over the throne, and when news reached Edinburgh that he had finally landed in Devon, a mob descended on Holyroodhouse and destroyed every item they could find with a Catholic connection.

Bonny Prince Charlie

Holyroodhouse became a lavish home for officers of state, who lived in luxury in the grace-and-favour apartments that were assigned to them. It had a brief renaissance as a palace in 1745, during Bonny Prince Charlie's doomed attempt to capture the throne for his father, the son of James II of England and VII of Scotland. The charismatic and romantic young prince held a glittering court at Holyroodhouse for five weeks in the autumn of 1745, but this was the final flowering of his Jacobite cause because it was eventually defeated at the Battle of Culloden in April 1746. Nevertheless, the cult of the Jacobites was considered to be so dangerous to national security that the wearing of highland dress was banned.

Rescued Again From Ruin

The gradual decline of Holyroodhouse continued, and when the roof of the abbey church collapsed in 1768 it was left as a ruin. Nevertheless, the palace slowly became an important venue on the eighteenth-century tourist trail, thanks to its vivid connections with Mary, Queen of Scots. The palace once again fulfilled its royal role in 1822 when George IV made a state visit to Scotland. However, Holyroodhouse was in such a sad and tatty state that George IV slept elsewhere, and only visited the palace for the state occasions that took place here.

As with so many other royal palaces that had been allowed to fade into gentle obscurity, Holyroodhouse was rescued and renovated by Queen Victoria. She enjoyed a life-long love affair with Scotland and was profoundly moved when she first visited the palace in 1850. Despite the palace's importance as an historic monument, Holyroodhouse still languished in a rather poor state of repair.

During the twentieth century, the importance and beauty of Holyroodhouse were finally recognized, and it was sympathetically modernized and restored. Today, Holyroodhouse is the official Scottish residence of the Queen, where she holds important state functions such as investitures, garden parties and summits. It is also the point where ancient converges with modern: the new Scottish Parliament building, a twenty-first century symbol of Scottish independence, stands next to the old Holyroodhouse, once the seat of a long line of Scottish monarchs.

BELOW: The King's Bedchamber lies at the centre of the palace. The overmantel painting is by Jacob de Wet, who also painted all the portraits in the Great Gallery.

GLAMIS CASTLE

The exterior of Glamis Castle, with its turrets, parapets and backdrop of the Grampian Mountains, is rich in atmosphere and magic. This is a castle steeped in Scottish history and redolent with legend. The interior of the castle, snug within its thick walls, is even more atmospheric, with an eerie, brooding quality. It is therefore highly appropriate that Glamis is alleged to be the most haunted stately home in Britain. A sturdy brother-in-law of the Queen Mother once claimed to have been pushed out of bed by a ghost, and there are reports of a ghost patrolling the Mad Earl's Walk on wild winter nights. There is also a grey lady who flits about the Chapel and a tongueless woman that runs across the grounds, clawing desperately at her mouth.

Another persistent rumour is that a member of the Bowes-Lyon family, which has owned Glamis for 600 years, was once walled up alive in a secret chamber, believed to be somewhere near the crypt (legend has it that there are more windows on the outside of the castle than can be found inside, hence the theory of secret rooms). One version on this theme claims that the poor soul was a monster whose existence had to be expunged from the family records. Nevertheless, each head of the family was apparently burdened with the knowledge of this ghastly secret. A variation of this story is that Earl Beardie, a fifteenth-century occupant, once played cards with the Devil on a Sunday and was walled up as a punishment. It is hardly surprising, therefore, that Shakespeare set Duncan's murder, at the hands of Macbeth, at Glamis, even though this is historically incorrect. How could he have resisted such a tempting piece of dramatic licence?

The Home of Kings

Glamis Castle was originally a hunting lodge for Scottish kings, and in 1034 Malcolm II died in the original castle after being fatally wounded in a battle. King Robert II gave the land to Sir John Lyon in 1372, in gratitude for services rendered; four years later, Sir John married Joanna, Robert's daughter, and was given a barony. His son, who was also called Sir John, began building what is now the east wing of the present castle in about 1400. The tower was added in 1440 and the castle was greatly extended in 1600, with further additions made later in the seventeenth century, in a style now called Scottish Baronial.

Throughout its life, Glamis Castle has always had strong links with Scottish history. One of its most sombre connections took place during the reign of King James V. Here was a man with a chip on his shoulder and the power with which to exact his revenge on whoever he felt deserved it. One focus of his bitterness was the Douglas family, into which his mother, Margaret Tudor, married after the death of her first husband, James IV, at the Battle of Flodden in 1513. The young King James V had a wretched childhood and never allowed himself, or anyone else, to forget it. James wrongly imprisoned Lady Janet Douglas, the widow of the 6th Lord Glamis, for witchcraft and she was eventually burned at the stake outside Edinburgh Castle. Her young son was also locked up, under sentence of death, and James confiscated Glamis Castle and lived here himself between 1537 and 1542. After James died on 14 December 1542, Parliament released the young 7th Lord Glamis and restored the castle to him, but by then many of its treasures were missing.

The Old Pretender

Glamis had a chequered history during the sixteenth and seventeenth centuries, thanks to the financial whims of its successive owners. By the time Glamis was restored to solvency in the late 1600s, its owners were styled the Earls of Strathmore and Kinghorne, and have been known as such ever since.

One of the most colourful royal visitors to the castle was the Old Pretender, James Francis Edward Stuart, who stayed here in February 1716. The exiled son of James II of England and VII of Scotland, he protested throughout his life that he was the rightful heir to the British throne, even to the point of being proclaimed James III of England and VIII of Scotland while in France in 1701. During his visit to Glamis, he participated in the ancient custom of 'touching for the King's Evil' in the Chapel. It was commonly believed that a true king or queen could successfully cure someone suffering from scrofula, or the King's Evil, simply by touching them. Much to the delight of his Jacobite supporters (and, presumably, the sufferers themselves), the Old Pretender duly proved his claim to the throne.

PAGE 130: The stairway from the front door leads to the vaulted crypt.

PAGE 131: The castle was remodelled in the early 1600s and the Drawing Room dates from this period. The ceiling was made by local craftsmen in 1621.

The Queen Mother

During the twentieth century, Glamis became famous as the ancestral home of Lady Elizabeth Bowes-Lyon, who married Prince Albert, Duke of York, in 1923. On the abdication of his brother, Edward VIII, Prince Albert unexpectedly succeeded to the throne as George VI in 1936. Elizabeth was the first Queen Consort to have been born in Britain since the reign of Henry VIII. In 1952, after George VI's death, she became known as HM Queen Elizabeth The Queen Mother, a position she occupied for almost exactly fifty years until her death on 30 March 2002.

Elizabeth was born in 1900 into an aristocratic, golden age that was obliterated by the mud of France during the First World War. Her fourteenth birthday coincided with the outbreak of war, during which Glamis was converted into a military hospital. Elizabeth rolled up her sleeves and helped to look after the many wounded soldiers who stayed here. Her duties were given added poignancy in 1915 when her brother, Fergus, was killed at the Battle of Loos. Two years later, it was feared that history was repeating itself when another brother, Michael, was reported missing in action; it was later

OPPOSITE: Duncan's Hall is so-named because it was once thought to be the site of his murder by Macbeth.

BELOW: The crypt was originally the lower hall, in which the castle servants ate and slept.

discovered that he had been taken prisoner of war. Throughout the rest of Elizabeth's life, as with so many of her generation, the First World War held special significance for her.

Pretty, amusing, charming and vivacious, the young Lady Elizabeth Bowes-Lyon was the most popular debutante in post-war London. She had a string of devoted admirers, the most notable being the Duke of York. Bertie, as his family knew him, was a shy, stammering young man who was plagued by nervous indigestion and dominated by his father, George V, who was a remote patrician. The sweet-natured young duke also had remarkable persistence, as he had to wait two years for Elizabeth to accept his marriage proposal. The Duke and Duchess of York, as they were known until 1936 when they became King George VI and Queen Elizabeth, regularly used the suite of three rooms at Glamis that are now called the Queen Mother's Apartments. They spent the latter half of their honeymoon at Glamis and their younger daughter, Princess Margaret, was born here in 1930. She was the first royal baby to have been born in Scotland since Charles I was born at Dunfermline Palace in 1600. Throughout her long and remarkable life, the Queen Mother always kept up her ties to her old family home, and these are now reciprocated by a special exhibition at Glamis in her memory.

LEFT: It is hardly surprising that so many legends are connected with Glamis Castle because it has such a potent atmosphere of mystery and magic.

ABOVE: The cover of the four-poster bed in the Queen Mother's Bedroom was embroidered by her mother, the 14th Countess of Strathmore and Kinghorne.

EDINBURGH CASTLE

Contemporary Edinburgh is a vibrant, busy city that deservedly attracts visitors from all over the world. There are modern shopping centres and the new Scottish Parliament building, symbolizing Scotland's new-found independence, is taking shape at the end of the Royal Mile. Yet there are still many reminders of ancient Edinburgh, from the claustrophobic, winding streets of the Old Town to the medieval Palace of Holyroodhouse, scene of one of the most notorious murders in Scottish history. With a little imagination one can almost smell the history: until the eighteenth century, what is now Princes Street Gardens was an uninviting, stinking stretch of water known as Nor' Loch, into which the city's waste and rubbish was thrown. Go back a thousand years further, and the two tallest points in Edinburgh were the lumpy Arthur's Seat, all that remains of a 340-million-year-old volcano, and the irregular outcrops of the castle rock, which were formed by ice sheets in the last Ice Age.

Battles with the English

This is the Edinburgh that King Malcolm III and Queen Margaret would have known in the eleventh century. Even then there was a royal palace, called the Castle of Maidens, on the castle rock. Although Malcolm acknowledged William the Conqueror as his overlord, this did not prevent William from invading northern England five times. On the fifth occasion, in November 1093, Malcolm was killed in battle at Alnwick. When his wife heard the news, she took to her bed and died a couple of days later. Four of their sons became kings of Scotland, but it was the youngest one, David I, who was responsible for turning Edinburgh Castle into an important royal palace. Among the buildings that were erected in his reign was St Margaret's Chapel, dedicated to his mother's memory, which is not only the oldest building in the castle but also in the whole of Edinburgh.

Most of the castle was built of timber, and as a result simply was not strong enough to withstand the assault mounted on it by Edward I in 1296 in the opening salvos of the Wars of Independence between the English and Scots. This began a 45-year period in which the English and Scots fought over the ownership of the castle, recapturing it by turns until it was wrenched from English hands for the last time in a bloody coup in 1341. By this time, the castle was uninhabitable, having been dismantled on the orders of Robert the Bruce in 1314 to stop it being used against him by the English, so his son, David II, had to rebuild the place. He built David's Tower, which now lies in ruins beneath the Half-Moon Battery, although parts of it are still accessible.

Crown Square

James III (1460–88) spent a large part of his reign at Edinburgh Castle, during which time he oversaw a great deal of building work. This included work on the Royal Palace that stood on the east side of the main courtyard of the castle, known at the time as Palace Yard but today called Crown Square. This courtyard housed the most important buildings in the castle: the Royal Palace, the Great Hall, the Royal Gunhouse and St Mary's church – unfortunately the latter two buildings no longer exist. The prettiness of Crown Square hides a secret: two tiers of stone cellars, known as the castle vaults, lie beneath it. These vaults have performed a variety of functions over the centuries, such as providing storage space for food and munitions, but they have also acted as military prisons, most notably for prisoners of war during the Napoleonic Wars at the turn of the nineteenth century.

PAGE 136: *The stained glass windows were added to St Margaret's Chapel in 1922.*

PAGE 137: *At night, the illuminated buildings of Edinburgh Castle dominate the skyline.*

Mary, Queen of Scots and the United Crown

The exposed position of Edinburgh Castle made it a cold and inhospitable place. After the reign of James III, succeeding Scottish monarchs much preferred the comfort of Holyroodhouse at the other end of the Royal Mile. In the spring of 1566, Mary, Queen of Scots was forced to take refuge in the Royal Palace in the castle as both her political and personal lives were in crisis and she feared for the safety of her unborn child. This child was safely delivered in the Birthchamber on the morning of 19 June, and grew up to become James VI of Scotland and I of England, uniting the crowns of two countries that had periodically been at war for centuries.

Mary was forced to abdicate her throne thirteen months later and her infant son, James VI, became king. Mary had a loyal supporter in Sir William Kirkcaldy of Grange, the governor of the castle, and, in 1571, he was involved in a protracted siege (known as the 'Lang Siege') against the regent who was ruling on behalf of the infant James. This siege finally ended in 1573 when Elizabeth I sent enough guns to ensure victory over the occupants of the castle. Sir William was executed in public.

James's succession to the English throne in 1603 unwittingly hastened the end of the castle's life as a royal residence, despite the fact that the Royal Palace was rebuilt during his reign. James might have been king of both England and Scotland, but the former

LEFT: The king spied on his courtiers through the opening on the right of the fireplace in the Great Hall.

BELOW: The aspidal chancel in St Margaret's Chapel is separated by an arch from the rectangular nave.

OPPOSITE: *The Laich Hall on the ground floor of the Royal Palace was created for the visit in 1617 of James VI of Scotland and I of England.*

LEFT: *The vaults beneath Crown Square have been used for storage of food and ordnance, and were also home to prisoners of war held during the American War of Independence (1775-83).*

was generally considered to be the more important country and it was also the seat of government. When James's son, Charles I, slept in the castle on the night before his Scottish coronation in June 1633, he was the last reigning monarch to do so. Charles was executed in 1649 and Britain became a republic. The crown passed to his son, Charles II, who was in exile in France at the time but was eventually crowned at Scone Abbey on 1 January 1651. Such strong Scottish support for the exiled king had already alerted Oliver Cromwell, who lost no time in setting up a powerful garrison in the castle. The army was permanently stationed here, and the defences strengthened.

The One O'Clock Gun

Edinburgh Castle once again came under fire at the start of the eighteenth century, during the five Jacobite Risings in support of the exiled James Francis Edward Stuart, popularly known as the 'Old Pretender'. A Jacobite attempt to capture the castle nearly succeeded in 1715 but failed due to a quirky combination of circumstances. After the 1745 Rising led by the Old Pretender's son, Bonny Prince Charlie, the castle's function as a defensive fortress has never again been put to the test. Nevertheless, a gun is still fired from the battlements in the Middle Ward each Monday to Saturday. This is the One O'Clock Gun, which is linked to the time-ball on top of the Nelson Monument on Calton Hill. When the gun fires, the time-ball drops, thereby providing a time-keeping signal for nearby shipping. It is one of the many reminders that, despite its popularity as a tourist attraction, the castle continues to play an important role in the daily life of Scotland's capital city.

STIRLING CASTLE

Should any visitor to Stirling Castle need to be reminded of one of the most important episodes in its long history and in that of Scotland, they have only to look north to the Wallace Monument that towers over the trees on Abbey Craig. This monument was erected in honour of William Wallace, who led the Scottish army to victory against the English at the Battle of Stirling Bridge in 1297. A statue of Wallace stands on a plinth on the monument, forever surveying the land that he protected.

Wallace would not recognize the castle that stands here today, as the present castle was built in the fifteenth century. The castle that Wallace knew was made from timber and has long since disappeared. We do not know when the first castle was built, but it had been established by the beginning of the 1100s when Alexander I of Scotland ordered that the chapel should be dedicated and endowed. He died at Stirling Castle in 1124.

A Strategically Prized Castle

Stirling Castle occupies the ideal defensive position, sitting on top of a massive rocky outcrop with panoramic views of the surrounding countryside. The Highlands rise behind it, the Lowlands stretch in front of it, and the River Forth runs beside it, flowing out to the Firth of Forth and the North Sea. The west face of the castle rock rises to 250 metres (820 feet), making it a formidable obstacle for any enemy. No wonder Stirling was such a prized possession to both the English and the Scots in the thirteenth and fourteenth centuries. Successive armies were prepared to fight for it, as whichever country owned the castle also exercised a powerful control, physical and psychological, over most of Scotland.

The castle soon became a pawn in the hands of power-hungry monarchs. When the Scots king, William the Lyon, was captured on his way to England in 1174, Stirling was one of the five Scottish castles that were demanded by the English as a ransom payment. The arrangement was revoked in 1189 and William died in the castle in 1214. This was the start of a long phase in which ownership of Stirling Castle switched between the English and Scots, usually to the accompaniment of much bloodshed. In 1296, it was far too great a prize for Edward I of England to resist, and he seized it after the Scots king, John Balliol, was deposed. Edward was a master of martial strategy and he appeared to take great delight in humiliating the Scots in the hope that this would prevent any more costly wars with them. However, he had more than met his match in William Wallace, who led the Scots army in conjunction with Andrew Murray. Wallace and Murray knew that the English troops would have to cross what was then a timber bridge at Stirling, and they simply watched and waited from their vantage point on

Abbey Craig. Their patience was rewarded when they mounted a successful ambush on 11 September 1297 and regained the castle. The Scots lost control of Stirling again the following year but recaptured it in 1299. By 1303, Edward I had gained control of almost every important Scottish castle except Stirling, so he mounted an ambitious campaign to win it back, succeeding in July 1304.

Bannockburn

Naturally, this state of affairs could not be allowed to last. Edward I died in 1307 and the English throne passed to his son, Edward II, who was anything but a masterful leader. The Scots, on the other hand, had lost their William Wallace (who had the dubious honour of being the first person to be hanged, drawn and quartered by the English) but gained a magnificent leader in Robert the Bruce, who became King of Scotland in 1306. His brother, Edward, besieged Stirling Castle in 1314 and gave the English army a deadline: if they failed to relieve the castle by 24 June they had to surrender it to the Scots. This was an unthinkable proposition to Edward II, and the opposing forces met on 23 and 24 June 1314 at the Battle of Bannockburn, which was won by the Scots. This magnificent victory is commemorated by a statue of Robert the Bruce on horseback, on the site of the battlefield near Stirling Castle.

Ownership of the castle switched once more from the Scots to the English in the late 1330s, and was not regained by the Scots until 1342, under the leadership of Robert the Steward. As Robert II, he later founded the Stewart (Stuart) dynasty of Scotland and England.

The Palace is Built

The building of the castle that we see today began during the reign of James IV (1488–1513), and included the Great Hall, the Forework and his personal residence, the King's Old Building. James IV was one of the great builders of the Stewart line, playing a major role in the architectural history of Edinburgh Castle, the Palace of Holyroodhouse, Falkland Palace and Linlithgow Palace. He would undoubtedly have carried out a great deal more building work at Stirling had he not been killed at the Battle of Flodden Field on 9 September 1513.

His infant son, James V, was crowned in the Chapel Royal at Stirling on 21 September 1513. His first bride was Princess Madeleine, the daughter of François I of France, but she died

PAGE 142: The painted decorations in the Chapel Royal were created by Valentine Jenkin for Charles I's visit in 1633.

PAGE 143: The gatehouse within the Forework has entries for pedestrians on either side of the main, arched entrance.

LEFT: The Grand Battery, with its row of cannons, was built in the Outer Close in 1689.

soon after their wedding in 1537. James's second wife was Mary of Guise, whom he married in 1538 and brought home to Scotland; he built the Palace within Stirling Castle for his new bride. The Palace is laid out around a central quadrangle known as the Lion's Den. The façades of the Palace are heavily ornamented with statues and carvings, which range from those of James V himself to gods, the Devil, animals and mythical beasts.

Coronations and Barracks

When James V died in December 1542, his baby daughter, Mary, became Mary, Queen of Scots. Like her father, she was crowned as a child at Stirling on 9 September 1543. It was the first time that the Honours of Scotland – the crown, sceptre and sword of state – were all used at a coronation. Mary had a chequered life, and she was forced to abdicate from the Scottish throne on 24 July 1567 in favour of her baby son, James VI. He was crowned at the Church of the Holy Rude, which was the parish church of the burgh of Stirling, on 29 July 1567 and spent much of his childhood at the castle. When James VI became James I of England in 1603 he moved to England and returned to Scotland only once, in 1617. Scottish castles, including Stirling, were allowed to fall into disrepair, only being renovated on the rare occasion when a monarch was due to visit. Stirling's defences were strengthened between 1708 and 1714, to counter the Jacobite Risings, which aimed to put James Stuart, the Old Pretender, on the throne.

During the Napoleonic Wars at the turn of the nineteenth century, the Great Hall at Stirling was converted into a barracks. The castle was later the base for the Argyll and Sutherland Highlanders until 1964, and there is a memorial to them on the Castle Esplanade. Today, much of the castle has been renovated to show its importance as an example of medieval and Renaissance architecture.

OPPOSITE: Although the castle was a fortress, it also offered recreation and relaxation in the form of its gardens.

ABOVE: Within the Inner Close, the King's Old Building stands at right angles to the Chapel Royal, which is to the right of the picture.

TRAQUAIR HOUSE

The oldest inhabited house in Scotland, Traquair House lies in a peaceful setting in the Borders. It has grown in size over the centuries as its inhabitants have built extra floors or wings, yet today it still has the feeling of a comfortable and much-loved family home. The Stuart family has lived at Traquair since 1478, when James III of Scotland gave the house to the Earl of Buchan, who in turn gave it to his son, James Stuart. He is an ancestor of the Maxwell Stuart family, who own Traquair today.

Royal Visitors

Originally, Traquair was a royal hunting lodge, as the surrounding countryside was rich in deer and other wildlife and provided good sport for the royal parties. The house, however, continued to have many royal visitors after it passed into the hands of the Stuart family, and it is claimed that, over time, 27 kings have visited Traquair. Mary, Queen of Scots, who particularly enjoyed hunting, stayed here in 1566 with her second husband, Lord Darnley. Her prayer book and rosary can still be seen here today.

HISTORY

- Tower built in the twelfth century
- Traquair House given to the Earl of Buchan in 1478 and passed to his son, James Stuart
- Mary, Queen of Scots visits during a hunting expedition in 1566
- Top floor built by John Stuart, 1st Earl of Traquair, in 1640s
- All Catholic objects destroyed by a mob in 1688
- Bonny Prince Charlie entertained at Traquair in 1745

OF SPECIAL INTEREST

- The museum, displaying the rosary and crucifix of Mary, Queen of Scots
- The Bear Gates, said to have remained shut since 1745
- The King's Room, where Mary, Queen of Scots stayed
- The First Library, restored to its original eighteenth-century appearance
- The Priest's Room and its secret staircase
- The brewery
- The gardens, including the old walled garden

Catholic Stuarts

Although the Scottish Crown made the Stuart family lairds, they never enjoyed the wealth and luxury of some of their fellow noblemen, thanks to their strong religious and political convictions. The family was Protestant until the 2nd Earl of Traquair converted to Catholicism in the mid seventeenth century, a time when the Catholic religion was regarded with great suspicion and fear by the State. Consequently, the Stuarts had to pay the heavy taxes that were levied on them as recusants, or people who refused to attend the religious services that had been established by law. Their problems were compounded after the Glorious Revolution of 1688, when James II, who had strong Catholic leanings, was forced to flee the country, leaving the throne vacant for his Protestant daughter and son-in-law, Mary II and William III.

Jacobite Sympathies

Supporters of the deposed James II, and later of his exiled son and grandson, popularly known as the Old Pretender and Bonny Prince Charlie respectively, were known as Jacobites and were considered to be profoundly dangerous subversives. The Stuarts fell into this category and, in 1688, a Protestant mob from Peebles ransacked Traquair, smashing every religious object they could find. The Jacobite sympathies of the 4th Earl landed him in prison in Edinburgh Castle during the 1715 Rising for the Old Pretender, and his son the 5th Earl spent two years in the Tower of London after taking part in the 1745 Rising of Bonny Prince Charlie. Indeed, it is said that the 5th Earl entertained Bonny Prince Charlie at Traquair itself. After he left, the 5th Earl locked the Bear Gates, which stand at the end of the avenue to Traquair, and swore that they would remain shut until a Stuart king was once again crowned in London.

The very difficult combination of being Catholic and Jacobite meant that the Stuarts could not afford to make many additions or improvements to Traquair from 1700 onwards. However, their loss has been our gain, as the house is full of wonderful period details and furnishings that might have been lost if subsequent generations of the family had been able to adapt the house to their changing needs.

PAGE 148, TOP: The bed in the King's Room is lavishly decorated.

PAGE 148, BOTTOM: The Drawing Room contains many portraits of members of the Maxwell Stuart family, who still live at Traquair.

PAGE 149: The exterior of Traquair, with its fairly small windows and massively thick walls, was dictated by necessity. Scottish winters were freezing and glass was expensive, so it made sense to make the windows big enough to let in light but not so large that they let in howling gales as well.

LEFT: Mary, Queen of Scots stayed in the King's Room in 1566. It is particularly memorable for the ornate decorations of the four-poster bed, as well as many other artefacts.

SCONE PALACE

After the Romans left Scotland, the area around Scone in Perthshire became a major Pictish stronghold. The Picts, or 'painted people', were subdued by Kenneth MacAlpin, who was half Pictish himself and who became King of the Picts in 843 and King of Scotland a couple of years later. There are suggestions that he brought the Stone of Destiny to Scone and set it on Moot Hill, where it became the crowning seat for coronations. The first recorded instance of a Scottish coronation was that of King Lulach in August 1057, who was crowned while seated on the Stone of Destiny at Scone.

In 1114, Alexander I founded an Augustinian priory at Scone, which became an abbey in 1169. This was the home of the Stone of Destiny when not in use as a coronation stone. The stone's provenance is hotly debated, with some authorities believing that it may be the stone, described in the Book of Genesis, on which Jacob rested his head at Bethel. But no matter where it came from, it exerted an irresistible attraction for Edward I of England in 1296. He was infuriated by the rebellion of John Balliol, the man he had appointed as the Scottish king (thus turning him into a lapdog) and who was now siding with the French against him. Edward's murderous army marched into Scotland and brought the country to its knees. Seizing the Stone of Destiny, Edward took it to Westminster Abbey; an act that symbolized what he saw as Scotland's subjugation by England. The stone stayed at Westminster Abbey until it was returned to Scotland and placed with due ceremony in Edinburgh Castle in 1996.

Changes in Ownership

Despite the absence of the Stone of Destiny, Scottish monarchs continued to be crowned at Scone Abbey. This tradition continued until Edinburgh became an increasingly important power-base in the fifteenth century, and the last purely Scottish king to be crowned at Scone was James IV in 1488. Nevertheless, in blatant defiance of the republic created by Oliver Cromwell after the execution of Charles I in 1649, the exiled Charles II was crowned King of Scotland at Scone in 1651. By this time, the original Scone Abbey had long since disappeared, having been burnt down in 1559, and had been replaced by Scone Palace. There had also been a change of ownership: in 1600, the land was given to Sir David Murray, the cupbearer of James VI. Sir David was an ancestor of the Earls of Mansfield who continue to live at Scone today.

A Nineteenth-Century Gothic Palace

Scone Palace underwent yet another transformation in 1803, by which time it was in a poor state. The 3rd Earl of Mansfield had it rebuilt as a gothic palace that echoed the old Scone Abbey and retained many of its medieval features. Unfortunately, due to misunderstandings between the architect, William Atkinson, and the clerk of works, much of the original building was lost, but nevertheless Scone Palace is a remarkably fine house with the evocative atmosphere of an earlier age.

ABOVE: The Drawing Room is full of treasures, including porcelain and two Boulle console tables.

RIGHT: Scottish parliaments met at Scone Abbey, where the palace now stands, between 1210 and 1452.

ALTHORP

Althorp, in Northamptonshire, has belonged to the highly influential Spencer family since it was first built in the sixteenth century. Sir John Spencer acquired the land in 1508 and used red brick to build a house there. The original shape of the building, which consists of a long range with two projecting wings, has formed the template for all subsequent alterations since then. Until the eighteenth century, despite various improvements and embellishments including converting the Elizabethan great hall into the Long Gallery and commissioning Le Nôtre, the French gardener, to landscape the grounds, the house periodically suffered from neglect as the family spent most of their time at their London home. The Spencers were powerful members of the Whig party, and the political climate of London held plenty to amuse them.

Saved from Ruin

It was the 2nd Earl Spencer, the main adviser of James II of England, who rescued Althorp from near ruin by commissioning the architect Henry Holland to remodel it in the late eighteenth century. At the time, Holland was also busily employed on what was to become the Royal Pavilion at Brighton and Carlton House in London, for the Prince of Wales. Today, the exterior of Althorp has changed little from Holland's original work, with the walls covered in rebate tiles to make the house more weatherproof. Inside, Holland moved the staterooms to the west wing and enlarged the Long Library. Althorp underwent further changes in 1877 when the State Dining Room was built and the Saloon was extended. In 1924, Spencer House in London was leased out and a great deal of the furniture was moved to Althorp. Although the house is particularly noted for its collection of art, including works by Lely, Van Dyck and Rubens, this is by no means all it has to offer to visitors.

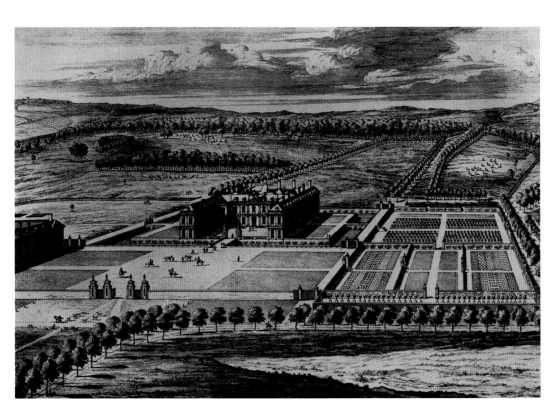

Lady Diana Spencer

The Spencer family is immensely well connected, having formed important dynastic links over the centuries with many other notable British families, including the Cavendishes (the Dukes of Devonshire) and the Churchills (the Dukes of Marlborough). On 29 July 1981, Lady Diana Spencer made one of the most glittering connections of all, when she married Prince Charles at St Paul's Cathedral in London.

Born on the Sandringham estate on 1 July 1961, Lady Diana was the daughter of the 8th Earl Spencer and the Hon. Mrs Shand-Kydd. Her father had been an equerry to George VI and Elizabeth II, and she grew up knowing the royal family. When her father succeeded to the title in 1975, the family moved out of Sandringham and into Althorp.

Although Althorp has long been an important stately home, it was the connection with the new Princess of Wales that brought it to the public's attention. Princess Diana was wildly popular in a manner that had not been seen since 1923 when Lady Elizabeth Bowes-Lyon married the Duke of York (they later became George VI and Queen Elizabeth). However, the media and public interest in Princess Diana became compulsive and intrusive, and at times it made her life a misery. Diana's marriage to Prince Charles ended in divorce on 28 August 1996 and, just over a year later, on 31 August 1997 she was killed in a car crash in Paris. After her funeral in Westminster Abbey on 6 September, she was buried on the island called the Oval at Althorp. Media speculation about her life, however, continues to rage.

OPPOSITE TOP: The present gardens were laid out in the 1860s by W. M. Teulon.

OPPOSITE, BOTTOM: This seventeenth-century engraving of Althorp shows the importance placed on the gardens and grounds, which were laid out by André Le Nôtre, who landscaped the gardens at Versailles.

ABOVE: When Henry Holland remodelled Althorp he chose to retain the tall Elizabethan chimneys.

Home sweet home to 35 monarchs.

London has some impressive homes – but none more so than these three Historic Royal Palaces.

The Tower of London [ABOVE], Kensington Palace [BELOW LEFT], Hampton Court Palace [BELOW RIGHT].

As a prison and place of execution, the Tower of London has been at the heart of Britain's history for over 900 years. Today you can see the breathtaking Crown Jewels and then explore the Tower's eventful past on a Yeoman Warder 'Beefeater' tour.

The working Tudor kitchens at Hampton Court Palace are as fascinating in their way as the splendid staterooms. Costumed guides will bring the past to life, and you can round off your day with a visit to the restored Privy Garden and the world-famous maze.

Kensington Palace is the most intimate of royal palaces. Home of William III and Mary II, it was the birthplace of Queen Victoria and the residence of Diana, Princess of Wales. On your visit you'll be able to walk through the majestic State Apartments and see the fascinating Royal Ceremonial Dress Collection.

BY BUYING A JOINT TICKET FOR TWO OR MORE OF THE PALACES YOU CAN SAVE MONEY. FOR ADVANCE BOOKINGS SEE THE WEBSITE OR CALL THE TOWER OF LONDON ON 0870 756 7070, HAMPTON COURT PALACE ON 0870 753 7777 OR KENSINGTON PALACE ON 0870 751 5180.

WWW.HRP.ORG.UK

KINGS AND QUEENS

KINGS AND QUEENS OF ENGLAND

THE HOUSE OF NORMANDY
1066-1087 William 1
1087-1100 William II
1100-1135 Henry I

THE HOUSE OF BLOIS
1135-1154 Stephen

THE HOUSE OF ANJOU OR PLANTAGENET
1154-1189 Henry II
1189-1199 Richard I
1199-1216 John
1216-1272 Henry III
1272-1307 Edward I
1307-1327 Edward II
1327-1377 Edward III
1377-1399 Richard II

THE HOUSE OF LANCASTER
1399-1413 Henry IV
1413-1422 Henry V
1422-1461 Henry VI

THE HOUSE OF YORK
1461-1470 Edward IV

THE HOUSE OF LANCASTER
1470-1471 Henry VI

THE HOUSE OF YORK
1471-1483 Edward IV
1483 Edward V
1483-1485 Richard III

THE HOUSE OF TUDOR
1485-1509 Henry VII
1509-1547 Henry VIII
1547-1553 Edward VI
1553 Lady Jane Grey
1553-1558 Mary I
1558-1603 Elizabeth I

KINGS AND QUEENS OF SCOTLAND

THE HOUSE OF DUNKELD
1058-1093 Malcolm III
1093-1094 Donald III
1094 Duncan II
1094-1097 Donald III and Edmund
1097-1107 Edgar
1107-1124 Alexander I
1124-1153 David I
1153-1165 Malcolm IV
1165-1214 William I
1214-1249 Alexander II
1249-1286 Alexander III
1286-1290 Margaret

1290-1292 The First Interregnum

THE HOUSE OF BALLIOL
1292-1296 John Balliol

1296-1306 The Second Interregnum

THE HOUSE OF BRUCE
1306-1329 Robert I
1329-1332 David II

THE HOUSE OF BALLIOL
1332 Edward

THE HOUSE OF BRUCE
1332-1333 David II

THE HOUSE OF BALLIOL
1333-1336 Edward

THE HOUSE OF BRUCE
1336-1371 David II

THE HOUSE OF STEWART
1371-1390 Robert II
1390-1406 Robert III
1406-1437 James I
1437-1460 James II
1460-1488 James III
1488-1513 James IV
1513-1542 James V
1542-1567 Mary, Queen of Scots
1567-1603 James VI (later James I of England)

KINGS AND QUEENS OF GREAT BRITAIN AND THE UNITED KINGDOM

THE HOUSE OF STUART
1603-1625 James I (James VI of Scotland)
1625-1649 Charles I

1649-1660 Commonwealth and Protectorate

THE HOUSE OF STUART (RESTORED)
1660-1685 Charles II
1685-1688 James II (James VII of Scotland)

THE HOUSE OF STUART AND ORANGE
1689-1694 William III and Mary II

THE HOUSE OF ORANGE
1694-1702 William III

THE HOUSE OF STUART
1702-1714 Anne

THE HOUSE OF HANOVER
1714-1727 George I
1727-1760 George II
1760-1820 George III
1820-1830 George IV
1830-1837 William IV
1837-1901 Victoria

THE HOUSE OF SAXE-COBURG-GOTHA
1901-1910 Edward VII

THE HOUSE OF WINDSOR
1910-1936 George V
1936 Edward VIII
1936-1952 George VI
1952- Elizabeth II

INDEX

and Anne Boleyn 18, 40-42, 62
grave at Windsor 14
Greenwich Palace 92-93
Hampton Court 18-21
Hever Castle 40-42
and Wales 98
Whitehall Palace 88
Hever Castle 40-43
Holland, Henry 30, 33
Althorp 154, 155
Holyroodhouse, Palace of 124-129
Houses of Parliament see Palace of Westminster
Howard, Catherine 63

I

Isabella, Queen 84
and murder of Edward II 112

J

Jacobite Risings 141, 147, 151
James I 21, 48, 119, 128, 139-140
Banqueting House 88
coronation 58
James II 74
abdication 66, 128, 151
James III of Scotland 136-137
James IV of Scotland 116, 122, 124
Stirling Castle 145
James V of Scotland 119
Falkland Palace 122-123
Glamis Castle 130
Holyroodhouse 124-125
Stirling Castle 145-147
James of St George 96-98, 102, 110
Jones, Inigo
Banqueting House 88, 89, 90
Queen's House 92-93

K

Katherine of Aragon 18, 40-41
Kensington Palace 4, 66-73
Kent, William 22
Kensington Palace 70, 71-72

L

Linlithgow Palace 8, 116-119
Llewelyn ap Gruffydd 96, 98, 102-105

Llewelyn ap Iorwerth 102
London Zoo 60

M

Magna Carta 112
Malcolm I of Scotland 136
Margaret, Princess 28, 29, 56, 66, 77
Marlborough, John Churchill, 1st Duke of 94, 106
Mary I 63
and Elizabeth I 48, 62
St James's Palace 74
Mary II 21, 90
Kensington Palace 66, 72
Mary of Guise 122-123, 124
Mary of Teck 34, 72, 121
Buckingham Palace 56
Sandringham 27, 28
Mary, Queen of Scots 119
abdication 138-139, 147
coronation 147
Edinburgh Castle 138-139
and Elizabeth I 126-127, 128, 139
Falkland Palace 123
Holyroodhouse 126-128
marriages 126-128
Stirling Castle 147
Traquair House 148
Midsummer Night's Dream 112
Moore, James 109
More, Sir Thomas 80
Mortimer, Roger
Berkeley Castle 110
and murder of Edward II 112
Myddelton, Sir Thomas 111

N

Nash, John
Buckingham Palace 54-55
Royal Pavilion 31, 33-34
St James's Palace 77
Norman Conquest see William I, 'the Conqueror'

O

Old Palace Yard 83
Order of the Garter 12
Ceremony *2, 13*
Osborne House *11*, 36-39
Owain Glyn Dwr 105

P

Palace of Holyroodhouse 124-129
Palace of Westminster *50-51*, 78-83
Parliament see Palace of Westminster
Parr, Katherine 21
Princes in the Tower 61-62
Princes of Wales 101

Q

Queen's House, The 92-93

R

Ralegh, Sir Walter 62, 64, 83
Reformation 40-41
Richard II 80, 84
Richard III 61-62
Rizzio, David 127
Robert the Bruce 145
Royal Menagerie 60
Royal Pavilion 30-35, 55
Rubens, Sir Peter Paul 88, 89, 90

S

St George's Chapel 12-14, *15*
St James's Palace 8, 74-77
Sandringham House 10, 24-29
Scone Palace *4*, 152-153
Seymour, Jane 21
Shakespeare, William 112, 130
Spencer, Lady Diana 28-29, 56-57, 155
Spencer Family 154-155
Stirling Castle 8, 142-147
Stone of Destiny 152
Stuart, Prince Charles Edward ('Bonny Prince Charlie') 116, 128, 151
Stuart, Prince James Francis ('Old Pretender') 132, 141, 147, 151
Stuart family 148-151

T

Thackeray, William 30
Tower of London *4*, 8, 58-65
Traitors' Gate 62
Traquair House 148-151
Trevisa, John 112

V

Vanbrugh, Sir John 106, 109
Verrio, Anthony 14
Victoria, Queen 8, 10, 129
Balmoral Castle 120-121
Buckingham Palace 55
children 24, 37-38
death 27, 39, 121
and death of Prince Albert 17, 24, 39, 55
Kensington Palace 68-69, 71, 72
Osborne House 36-39
Royal Pavilion 34
Windsor Castle 14, 17
Victoria Tower Gardens 83

W

Wallace, William 142, 143-145
Wars of the Roses 12, 61, 105
Webb, Sir Aston 56
Westminster Abbey 78
Westminster Hall 78-80
Westminster, Palace of *50-51*, 78-83
Whitehall Palace 8, 66, 88
see also Banqueting House
William I, 'the Conqueror' 8, 12, 44, 58
and Northern England 136
Palace of Westminster 78
William II 58
Palace of Westminster 78-79
William III 14, 90
death 21
Hampton Court Palace 21, 22, 23
Kensington Palace 66, 70
William IV 34, 55
Kensington Palace 69
St James's Palace 77
Windsor Castle 2, 8, 10, 12-17, *16-17*
Wolsey, Thomas 8, 18
World War II 56
Wren, Sir Christopher
Hampton Court Palace 21, 22, 23
Kensington Palace 66, 70
Wyatt, James 33
Windsor Castle 14

159

ACKNOWLEDGEMENTS & USEFUL ADDRESSES

Many thanks to Chris Coe and Paul Riddle for their stunning photography; to Historic Royal Palaces, the charitable Trust that manages HM Tower of London, Hampton Court Palace, Kensington Palace and the Banqueting House at Whitehall; to everyone at New Holland who worked on this book but especially Jo Hemmings, Jane Morrow, Deborah Taylor and Charlotte Judet; to Maggie Rothwell and Jean Struthers for lending me books; and to Chelsey Fox and Bill Martin for their behind-the-scenes support.

All photographs taken by Chris Coe, with the exception of the following: © Andy Williams p2, p6, p13, p15, p24, p26, p30, p31, p115, p120, p121. © Paul Riddle Architectural Photographer p32, p35, p40, p41, p42, p43, p48, p49, p50, p92, p93, p154, p155. © Paul Riddle Architectural Photographer and Historic Royal Palaces p18, p19, p20, p22, p23, p58, p59, p60, p61, p62, p63, p64, p65, p66, p67, p68, p69, p70, p71, p72, p88, p89, p90, p91. © Sandringham Estate, photographs by gracious permission of H.M. The Queen, p25, p29. The Royal Collection © 2003, Her Majesty Queen Elizabeth II, p16, p17 (Mark Fiennes), p52 (John Freeman), p53, p57 (Derry Moore), p75, p76 (Jeremy Whitaker), p126, p129 (Antonia Reeve). © Blenheim Palace, reproduced by kind permission of His Grace the Duke of Marlborough, p95, p106 (Chris Andrews), p107, p108 (Chris Andrews), p109. Pictures of Caernarfon and Harlech Castles by kind permission of Cadw.

Windsor Castle and St George's Palace
Windsor, Berkshire, SL4 INJ
+44 (0)8707 515175
www.windsor.gov.uk/attractions/castle

Hampton Court Palace
East Molesey, Surrey, KT8 9AU
+44 (0)8707 527777
www.hrp.org.uk

Sandringham House
Norfolk, PE35 6EN
+44 (0)1533 772655
www.sandringhamestate.co.uk

The Royal Pavilion
Brighton, BN1 1EE
+44 (0)1273 290900
www.royalpavilion.org.uk

Osbourne House
East Cowes, Isle of Wight, PO32 6JY
+44 (0)1983 200022
www.english-heritage.org.uk

Hever Castle
Hever Castle, Edenbridge, Kent, TN8 7NG
+44 (0)1732 865224
www.hevercastle.co.uk

Carisbrooke Castle
Castle Hill, Newport, Isle of Wight, PO30 1XY
+44 (0)1983 523112
www.english-heritage.org.uk

Hatfield Palace
Hatfield, Hertfordshire, Al9 5NQ
+44 (0)1707 262823
www.hatfield-house.co.uk

Buckingham Palace
Buckingham Palace Road, London, SW1
+44 (0)207 766 7300
www.royal.gov.uk

The Tower of London
London, EC3
+44 (0)870 7526 6060
www.hrp.org.uk

Kensington Palace
Kensington Gardens, London, W8
+44 (0)870 751 5170
www.royal.gov.uk

St James's Palace
See Buckingham Palace

The Palace of Westminster
Parliament Square, London, SW1
+44 (0)7219 3000
www.parliament.uk

Eltham Palace
Court Yard, London, SE9
+44 (0)8294 2548
www.english-heritage.org.uk

The Banqueting House
Whitehall, London, SW1
+44 (0)870 751 5178
www.hrp.org.uk

The Queen's House
Romney Road, Greenwich, SE10
+44 (0)20 8858 4422
www.nmm.ac.uk

Caernarfon Castle
Castle Ditch, Caernarfon, Gwynedd, LL5 2AY
+44 (0)1286 677617
www.caernarfon.com

Harlech Castle
Castle Square, Harlech, Gwynedd, LL46 2YH
+44 (0)1766 780552
www.harlech.com

Blenheim Palace
Woodstock, Oxfordshire OX20 1PX
+44 (0)8700 602080
www.blenheimpalace.com

Chirk Castle
Chirk, Wrexham, LL14 5AF
+44 (0)1691 777701
www.chirk.com/castle

Berkeley Castle
Berkeley, Gloucestershire, GL13 9BQ
+44 (0)1453 810332
www.berkeley-castle.com

Linlithgow Palace
Kirkgate, Linlithgow, West Lothian EH49 7AL
+44 (0)1506 842896
www.historic-scotland.gov.uk

Balmoral Castle
Ballater, Aberdeenshire, AB35 5TB
+44 (0)13397 42534
www.balmoralcastle.com

Falkland Palace
Falkland, Cupar, KY15 7BU
+44 (0)1337 857397
www.nts.org.uk

The Palace of Holyroodhouse
Holyrood Road, Edinburgh EH8 8AE
+44 (0)131 556 5100
www.royal.gov.uk

Glamis Castle
Glamis, by Forfar, Angus, DD8 1RJ
+44 (0)1307 840393
www.strathmore-estates.co.uk

Edinburgh Castle
The Royal Mile, Edinburgh, EH1 2NG
+44 (0)131 225 9846
www.historic-scotland.gov.uk

Stirling Castle
Castle Wynd, Stirling, FK8 1EJ
+44 (0)1786 450000
www.historic-scotland.gov.uk

Traquair House
Traquair House, Innerleithen, Peebleshire, EH44 6PW
+44 (0)1896 830323
www.traquair.co.uk

Scone Palace
Perth, PH2 6BD
+44 (0)1738 552300
www.scone-palace.net

Althorp
Northampton, NN7 4HQ
+44 (0)1604 772110
www.althorp.com